RELICS OF WAR IN Northumberland

Exploring Military Remains in the Landscape

Ian Hall

First published in the United Kingdom in 2020 by Northern Heritage Services Limited

Northern Heritage Services Limited
Units 7 & 8 New Kennels, Blagdon Estate, Seaton Burn,
Newcastle upon Tyne NE13 6DB

Telephone: 01670 789 940

www.northern-heritage.co.uk

See our full online catalogue at www.northern-heritage.co.uk

Copyright ©Ian Hall

ISBN: 9781916237629

Typeset in PT Sans

Design and layout by Ian Scott Design

Printed by Martins the Printer, Berwick-upon-Tweed

British Library Cataloguing in Publishing Data
A catalogue record for this book is available from the British Library

All photographs taken by the author unless otherwise stated

Contents

Introduction

Like all of Britain, Northumberland was profoundly affected by the Second World War. From the very beginning, the county was very much on the front line with its east facing coast making it a prime invasion target. Despite being a quiet rural county, remote from major industrial centres, it took part in the massive construction programme that was to dominate the British landscape for the duration of the war.

By 1945, Northumberland, like most parts of the country, had a wide range of military facilities. Airfields, radar stations and invasion defences had sprung up across the countryside, all part of the drive to satisfy the needs of the Armed Forces. With the end of the war in Europe, the vast majority of these sites were rapidly decommissioned as the serving men and women were demobilised, though a few were retained as the short-lived peace turned into the Cold War. While some of the constructions were dismantled, much was left in place. Farmers were, for example, paid £5 to remove each pillbox on their land, though, in practice, most of them just took the money and kept the pillboxes! The sturdiness of the concrete and the lack of pressure on the land for development has ensured their survival to the present day.

The concrete anti-tank cubes that can be found on many of the county's beaches are perhaps the most recognisable of these relics, but there is so much more to be discovered. Neglected for many years, it is perhaps now time for the reminders of this important period in our nation's history to be better understood, and properly preserved for the future.

Much has already been written about this period of the county's wartime history, most of it relating to the experiences of the people living here at the time. In contrast, little has been written about the tangible remains that exist in the landscape. My 2013 booklet, *Relics of War,* was an attempt, in a small way, to remedy this. I followed up with two more booklets; *Most Secret* told the story of the county's Auxiliary Units, while *Spitfires Over Northumberland* dealt mainly with pilot training at Eshott and Boulmer. In writing this new book I have naturally drawn from these books and have also added in new material unearthed since the publication of each of the previous titles.

This then is a guide to the various wartime remains that are to be found within the modern boundary of the county of Northumberland. It is not a history of the war itself; there are many excellent histories already out there which make that unnecessary. Instead, this is an attempt to describe what can be seen and what its purpose was. In writing the book, I have opted not to take a chronological approach, but instead have covered each category of relic in a separate chapter. There are therefore separate chapters to cover the subjects of Fighter Command Airfields, Radar sites, Anti-invasion defences, Auxiliary Units and Training Airfields, the order being approximately chronological from their first appearance in Northumberland. Appendices have been included to add more detail in some specific areas. Much use is made of real examples that can be seen in the landscape, and I have concentrated, wherever possible, on those that are readily accessible without trespassing on private land.

Most people who get involved in researching the subject of wartime remains are surprised by the lack of official records. Some work may never have been properly recorded, perhaps due to the speed with which works were built. Of the records that did exist, many will have been destroyed in the intervening years, with others perhaps lost in the depths of some archive, awaiting rediscovery. A lot of what we know, therefore, has come from individuals walking the landscape and recording what they found. Of particular note is the Defence of Britain Project, carried out in between 1995 and 2001, where volunteers sent in information about known structures. This provided the best picture to date of the construction work carried out during the war. A map of the county's extant pillboxes, for example, reveals once again the planning that was involved in the anti-invasion defences of 1940.

While the data in the Defence of Britain project initial research did suffer from some inaccuracies – for example, map references were often incorrect, and there was duplication as different volunteers recorded the same site – over the past few years, organisations such as the Pillbox Study Group have worked hard to review and refine information. It has to be said, however, that the records are still incomplete, and new relics are still being found.

It is important to make the point that most of the structures mentioned in this book have not been maintained since they were abandoned and as such can be in a poor, or even unstable, condition. Proper care should be taken when approaching them. It is also important to obtain the landowners permission before visiting those sites which are not either on a public right of way, or on open access land. For anyone interested in exploring from the comfort of their armchair, I can recommend Google Earth and the online Ordnance Survey mapping system – many of the relics mentioned are visible on these sites.

I have included a gazetteer which provides the locations of the most important remains, including those mentioned in the text. It is not, however, a complete listing of all known sites. One aspect which I have brushed over is the specific locations of the Auxiliary Unit underground bases. Information is in the public domain for these, but they are all on private land and are now so fragile that I feel all visits are best avoided until such a time as they can be better protected in some way.

Ian Hall

Acknowledgments

It is important that I acknowledge the following people who have helped me in my explorations and research. Colin Anderson and Stephen Lewins, both of the Pillbox Study Group, who have regularly contributed their wide knowledge, Bill Ricalton and Phil Rowett for their help with the Auxiliary Units and Chris Davies for his help relating to aircraft and airfields.

The Supermarine Spitfire Mk 1 was a common sight in the skies of Northumberland during WW2, operating regularly from Acklington, Boulmer, Eshott and Ouston.

The Hawker Hurricane Mk 1 was the mainstay of the RAF during the Battle of Britain. Less often seen over Northumberland, it did operate periodically from both Acklington and Ouston.

Fighter Command

It can be claimed, with some justification, that the single most pivotal moment of the Second World War was the Battle of Britain, fought principally (but not entirely) in the skies over southern England during the summer of 1940. The victory of 'the few' against the superior forces of the Luftwaffe ensured that the planned invasion of Britain, Operation Sealion, never took place. If Britain had fallen at that time, or if it had been forced to seek terms with Nazi Germany, any liberation of the continent of Europe was likely to be a long time coming. It was indeed the RAF's greatest moment.

The RAF, as an independent service, was born in the last few months of the Great War, formed from the merger of the Royal Navy Air Service (RNAS) and the Army's Royal Flying Corps (RFC). Even as it was formed, the military were still learning to exploit what was a new technology. It must be remembered that the first powered flight by the Wright brothers only occurred in 1903. When WW1 broke out, most people had never even seen an aeroplane, a situation that would soon change. Even in Northumberland, so far in the north, the local people would become familiar with aeroplanes in the skies above their county. From almost the start of the war, the RNAS operated seaplanes from a number of bases on the coast, including Seahouses and Holy Island, while airships operated from Chathill and Cramlington, all mainly employed in searching for enemy shipping.

Very soon, however, Britain was faced with a new threat, one which would shape much of the future military strategy. The German Navy's airship fleet, mainly based on the Zeppelin, started to carry out bombing from the air. Targets tended to be industrial, but with very limited bombing accuracy, inevitably residential areas were also hit. On 14th April 1915, Northumberland suffered what was only the second ever air raid on Britain, with the target being the south-east of the county and Tyneside. As the number of attacks across the country increased, there was an urgent need to develop some form of defence. The main response was for the RFC to create Home Defence squadrons which would be based along the eastern coasts of the country, which were the areas most under threat from the airships.

Locally, the RFC operated aeroplanes from a number of bases in the county. Initially based at Cramlington, they later relocated to Ashington and New Haggerston. As well as these three main airfields, there were also an additional ten smaller night landing fields which provided alternative landing places for

Concrete bomb store at the WW1 Ashington airfield

refuelling and rearming. Although the RFC had limited success in destroying the airships, their presence forced them to fly ever higher, and to abort missions sooner, so they were effective in dealing with the threat. Latterly the airships were withdrawn, and the bombing raids started to be carried out by large biplane aircraft, though Northumberland was well beyond the range of these bombers.

At the end of hostilities, in 1918, the RAF was rapidly cut back. Locally, all the airfields in Northumberland were closed and the land returned to agriculture. Little remains today to be seen, apart from Ashington, where the remains of a small concrete building survive. This is believed to have been a bomb store. A cross shaped wood adjacent to what was the landing field is thought to have been planted as an aid to navigation for the pilots.

It is worthwhile noting that the Zeppelin raids, while not causing major loss of life (certainly as compared to the air raids of WW2), created the foundations for the national air defence system which would be used so successfully in the next war. Without this system, it is distinctly probable that the RAF would have been overwhelmed by the superior forces of the Luftwaffe and not have won the Battle of Britain. It wouldn't have been seen so at the time, but the Zeppelin raids were perhaps a blessing in disguise.

The reduced RAF would continue operating for the next 15 years with minimal

Ashington airfield form the air

investment, carrying out its main role of policing the more remote regions of the Empire and providing regular air displays at home. Aircraft design progressed only slowly. Even as late as the mid-1930s, the aircraft that were in service would be recognisable in their similarity to those being used at the end of WW1.

Meanwhile fears were arising regarding the remilitarisation that was being carried out in Germany. This raised the spectre of aerial bombing that had first been experienced during WW1. It was realised that the performance of the RAF's silver painted fighter biplanes, such as the Bristol Bulldog and Gloster Gauntlet, was hardly any better than that of the bombers that were being developed by Germany. Stanley Baldwin famously said in parliament in 1932 that "the bomber will always get through", and it was generally considered that whole cities would be reduced to dust through bombing from the air, a fear only reinforced following the infamous German bombing of Guernica during the Spanish Civil War. The lack of adequate air defences became more critical. So, it was against the background of the threat of aerial attack and the rising menace from the militarisation of Nazi Germany that Britain belatedly started, in the mid-1930s, a programme of expansion of the RAF.

New airfields were constructed, both as operational bases and for training. At the same time, new aircraft and engine designs were progressed, most famously, the Supermarine Spitfire and Hawker Hurricane fighters and the Rolls Royce

Merlin engine. Interestingly, all three of these projects were started as private ventures with the development costs only being taken on by the government at a later date.

The period of pre-war airfield building has been called the 'expansion phase'. The sites followed a similar design, with all the accommodation and technical areas being grouped together on one side of the large grass airfield. By the time war broke out, the new 'expansion' airfields were being built with hard runways, and the older airfields' grass landing fields were being updated.

On the outbreak of war, the RAF's airfields (along with radar sites) were given priority for the very limited supplies of anti-aircraft guns which were vital for defence against air attack. In addition, airfields near the east coast, which were seen as potential landing sites for airborne troops during an invasion, were provided with a range of defences to repulse such an attack. Perimeter pillboxes were built, often with their main embrasures facing towards the airfield, while a Battle HQ bunker, in a position overlooking the airfield, would be used to coordinate the airfield's defence operations.

The RAF's airfields also became involved in the massive programme of decoy building that was used as a defence for strategic sites. In an attempt to reduce the effectiveness of bombing raids, imitation facilities were built to try and steer attacking aircraft away from their real target. This approach, when used to protect major industrial targets, adopted the name Starfish. For airfields to deal with daylight attacks, imitation runways were painted on a grass field, and RAF personnel were employed to move plywood aircraft around the site to impersonate an operational airfield. Known as a K type decoy, they had limited success, particularly because, following the Battle of Britain, the Luftwaffe bombing raids increasingly moved to night-time therefore the decoys were not visible. As a result, the K-sites fell into disuse and new decoys, known as Q-sites, were developed, which used lighting effects to imitate the flare path and taxiing aircraft of an active airfield at night. These sites were simpler to operate, requiring a staff of just two, with a simple control room with adjacent generator house. Also, the lighting arrays were such that the land could still be farmed which was an increasingly important issue, with food being so scarce.

RAF Acklington

The first new airfield in Northumberland was RAF Acklington, which opened in 1938. A typical expansion phase airfield, it was built on the site of a WW1 landing field, Southfields, and was originally planned as an armament training camp, using the newly opened range at Druridge Bay. On the outbreak of war, however, it was transferred to Fighter Command where it became the North East's main fighter base during the Battle of Britain.

Acklington didn't have any permanent resident squadrons. As with most Fighter Command airfields in the north, it was mainly used to provide some respite for squadrons who had seen intense action over the Channel and southern England. These relocated units were still used operationally in the North East, however, defending against enemy raids. The lack of a hard runway at Acklington in the early months did cause problems. In the spring of 1940, the resident squadron had to revert to using outdated Gloster Gladiator biplanes as its Spitfires were unable to use the grass runways, such was their poor condition. Thankfully, Acklington would soon get hard runways.

On 15th August 1940, the Luftwaffe launched a large number of raids on targets across Britain. This was intended to be the knock-out blow in preparation for Operation Sealion, the planned invasion of Britain. Attacks were planned on the Forth and Tyne areas from bases in Norway, using a force of 65 Heinkel He 111 bombers and 34 Messerschmidt Bf 110 fighter escorts. Detected by radar, including the Chain Home station at Ottercops Moss, near Elsdon, the Spitfires of Acklington's 72 Squadron were amongst the aircraft that intercepted the German raiders, inflicting major losses, which were exacerbated as the attackers, expecting all of the RAF's forces to be in the south, left out many of the rear gunners in the Bf 110 escorts in order to save weight and so increase their range.

Pilot Officer Robert Elliot, of 72 Squadron, recorded how the Spitfires had the advantage of height when the raiders were spotted. He wrote "I do not think they saw us to begin with. When they did, the number of bombs jettisoned was fantastic. You could see them falling away from the aircraft and dropping into the sea, literally by the hundreds. The formation became a shambles." In the story of the Battle of Britain, 15th August became known as Black Thursday due to the Luftwaffe losses. Significantly, the Luftwaffe never launched another major daylight raid on the north.

RAF Acklington operated throughout the war, hosting a wide range of squadrons, including night fighting Mosquitos.

After the war, Acklington continued in operation as an RAF base, eventually becoming the base for the Air Sea Rescue helicopters of 202 squadron. It was finally closed in 1972, when the helicopters were transferred to RAF Boulmer. After closure, much of the airfield was open cast mined, while the main site was converted to a prison, now HMP Northumberland.

There are a series of four pillboxes that were built to provide a defence for the airfield. Three of these pillboxes have been modified to provide a walled anti-aircraft (AA) gun position on top, and one of these is easily accessible from an adjacent public footpath.

There is also a group of buildings which are believed to have been a VHF direction finding site, which would have helped to direct aircraft back to base.

Some of the old perimeter track is still in place, though it is all on private land, and there is a hangar within the prison perimeter, though this is clearly not accessible!

Acklington was provided with a dual 'K' and 'Q' decoy at Boulmer. Today, nothing remains of either of these decoy sites. Later, with the Boulmer site being

RAF Acklington type 22 pillbox with roof mounted light anti-aircraft gun position

RAF Acklington VHF site

RAF Acklington Q type decoy control building

converted into a training airfield, a new 'Q' type decoy was built near Widdrington. The control building for this can be seen from the A1068.

Nearby, at the cemetery at Chevington can be found the graves of some of the pilots who died while serving at both RAF Acklington and RAF Eshott. There are also a number of graves for German aircrew who died after being shot down over the county. All of these graves are being well cared for by the Commonwealth War Graves Commission.

Commonwealth War Graves at Chevington

RAF Ouston

In 1941, a second Northumberland operational fighter airbase was opened near Harlow Hill. As with Acklington, this was an 'expansion period' layout, though this had hard runways from the outset. The layout of the three runways is interesting as they all intersect at about the same location, making them all vulnerable to a bombing strike. After the war, RAF Ouston became a base for the Auxiliary Air Force, and in 1974 it was passed over to the Army to become Albemarle Barracks. This site is still operational and as a result, the main airfield cannot be visited.

There are, however, a few remains outside the current site's boundary which can be visited. As with other airfields of this period, it was well defended, with a

RAF Ouston airfield defence pillbox

Brick-lined fire trench at RAF Ouston

RAF Ouston VHF site

number of pillboxes being built around the perimeter, at least nine of which still exist. Many of these are of an unusual design, including a number of circular types. In particular, Harlow Hill, to the south of the airfield was well defended, with at least four pillboxes and a number of brick lined fire trenches.

There are also two separate sites which are assumed to be related to VHF direction finding.

Ouston was also provided with a 'Q' type decoy at Berwick Hill near Ponteland of which the control building survives.

RAF Ouston Q type decoy control building

Radar

The story of radar is a fascinating tale of technical innovation, where new designs emerged almost continuously, and systems were commissioned that had already been overtaken by newer developments. The first system was in place just in time for the start of the war. Within a couple of years, a whole range of radar systems were protecting our skies. By this time, radar was also being fitted to aircraft and ships, while other systems were being used to direct the fire of guns. In considering the remains that can be found in Northumberland, however, the following relates only to the developments in the field of air defence, an area where the county still has a central role with the RAF bases at Boulmer and Brizlee Wood. Interestingly, Northumberland is one of only four counties that has had a continuous RAF radar presence from the outbreak of war to the present day.

The need to be able to detect the presence of enemy aircraft as quickly as possible was brought home to the British authorities during the Great War with the German bombing raids. It was clear that any realistic countermeasures to these attacks required the location of any attacker to be determined as far in advance as possible to enable warnings to be given to civilians on the ground, artillery defences to be prepared and fighter aircraft to be got airborne early enough to have a reasonable chance of intercepting the raiders. During WW1, and indeed through to the mid-1930s, early warning was dependent upon sight and sound, and it was this need that led to the creation of the Royal Observer Corps. In particular, much effort was made to try and develop an effective sound location system, with the main efforts being based on large concrete 'sound mirrors'. Official prototypes were built at several locations along the south-east coast, and a number of private ventures were tried in the north, including one at Fulwood near Sunderland. Despite some promising signs, however, in the end, sound detection proved to be a technical dead-end and an effective system was never put into operation.

The breakthrough came on 26th February 1935 when a small team led by Robert Watson-Watt was able to demonstrate the viability of detecting aircraft using reflected radio waves. This first test famously used the transmissions from the BBC transmitter at Daventry to detect an RAF bomber. The Air Ministry was convinced, and a rapid development programme started.

By the outbreak of war Britain had an operational radar system that covered the whole of the east coast, from the south of England to the north of Scotland.

Fulwell sound mirror

Typical Chain Home radar site, at Poling Sussex [public domain]

Named Chain Home (CH), there was one site in Northumberland at Ottercops Moss near Elsdon. The neighbouring sites in the chain were, to the south, Danby Beacon, and to the north, Drone Hill, near Coldingham.

CH stations covered a large area. The first CH sites comprised of four 360-foot-high self-supporting steel transmitting towers, erected in a line parallel to the coast. Later sites, such as Northumberland's Ottercops Moss, would have three transmitting towers. The transmitters emitted a regular pulse of radio energy which would 'floodlight' the sky. Any reflections from aircraft would be detected by an array of four 240-foot-high wooden towers, arranged in a rhomboid shape, and built to one side of the transmitters. The time from transmission to receiving the reflection gave the distance to the target, while the relative strength of the reflected signal on each face of the receiving array could be used to work out the direction of the target. An Identification Friend or Foe (IFF) system enabled RAF and enemy aircraft to be identified separately. As CH expanded around to the west coast, the towers were usually replaced with guyed masts.

CH was integrated into a sophisticated air defence system whereby radar and visual reports from the Royal Observer Corps were coordinated in order to provide clear information to airfields and pilots, anti-aircraft guns, searchlights and civilian air raid warnings. Named the Dowding System, after its inventor, the RAF's Sir Hugh Dowding, it proved decisive during the Battle of Britain, where it enabled the RAF to maximise the effect of its limited aircraft and aircrew.

The size of the CH sites, and in particular the large towers, made them very vulnerable to Luftwaffe raids. This prompted the construction of underground reserve transmitting and receiving stations, with smaller aerials, which would provide a limited back-up to the main over-ground facilities in case they were put out of action.

Although CH had many disadvantages – for example the sites required a large staff and the low-level performance was limited – what the system did have was range. CH could 'see' a long way, and this kept it in operation throughout the war, and even, for some sites, into the early years of the Cold War.

Meanwhile, as one team was busy developing CH, another group was looking at how the technology might be used to detect ships. This led to a system called Coastal Defence (CD). This started to be deployed from 1940 and used two aerials, one for transmitting and the other for receiving. These were turned in unison to find targets. CD's range was much less than CH, but once in operation it was found that the system was also good at detecting low level aircraft, something that was a blindspot for CH. As a result, the system was taken up for air defence as well, being named Chain Home Low (CHL). These two types were quickly brought together as CD/CHL. Further developments improved performance resulting in the Chain Home Extra Low (CHEL) system, which used tall towers for mounting the aerials to further improve detection ranges.

In Northumberland CD sites were built at Spittal (near Berwick), Craster, Amble and Hartley Crag (near Seaton Sluice). CHL sites were built at Bamburgh and Cresswell. Later, the CD/CHL sites at Bamburgh, Craster and Cresswell were upgraded to CHEL.

The main problem with all these radar systems, however, was the difficulty in tracking multiple targets and in directing fighter aircraft to intercept enemy raiders. This was solved, however, in 1942, with the introduction of Ground Control Intercept (GCI) radar. This system had a combined transmitting and receiving aerial which continuously rotated, with the information from this being displayed on a circular screen which would show all aircraft in the vicinity, something that is familiar with us today. This allowed controllers to easily direct fighters to any enemy aircraft so increasing the likelihood of a successful interception. A temporary GCI station was opened at Dinnington. Later, a permanent GCI station was opened at Northstead, near Widdrington. After the war, the equipment was moved to Boulmer, and the Northstead site was lost when the area was open cast mined.

Ottercops Moss

The Ottercops Moss Chain Home site was originally planned to be built at Steng Cross, where Winter's Gibbet stands, but objections from various landowners led to the planning application being refused, with secrecy at this time preventing the War Department being able to inform the public about the critical nature of this installation. The site was therefore moved a few miles to the south which created so many problems due to the waterlogged nature of the ground that the station was one of the last ones of the first phase to be opened. The site was so wet that there were problems in fixing foundations for the towers, and underground structures were prone to flooding, a problem that was never really solved during the life of the station.

Today, the radar towers are long gone, but there are many other remains to be seen and the site is well worth exploring. As with all CH stations, Ottercops Moss was well defended from attack, either by bombing, or even by raiding from parachutists. There was an outer perimeter defence, with four type 22 pillboxes positioned at the extremities . Three of these pillboxes were adjacent to light anti-aircraft (LAA) positions, fitted with the 40mm Bofors gun. The foundations

Ottercops Moss type 22 pillbox, protecting one of the anti-aircraft gun positions

Inside one of the Ottercops Moss type 22 pillboxes

Ottercops Moss type 24 pillbox

of one of these positions, together with the base of a hut, remain. These were manned by the regular Army. Their graffiti, including names and regiments, can be seen on the inside of the pillboxes. There are also some markings which give the distance to landmarks which would have helped the occupants determine the range of any attacking force.

An inner defensive perimeter was created by eight type 24 shellproof pillboxes, though these are all in a poor condition following a failed post-war attempt at demolition.

The reserve transmitting and receiving stations can be seen. These each have two concrete sliding roofs, the larger being for equipment installation and the smaller for personnel access, and the bases for the temporary aerials can be found close by.

Ottercops Moss underground reserve station

Apart from the defences, there are other buildings surviving. As with all the early CH sites which were built before the outbreak of war, they were expected to be on standby until such as time as hostilities broke out. Each site therefore had a warden's house, where a caretaker would live and keep the site in readiness.

Sewage plant, with warden's house and guard post, at Ottercops Moss

This house is now a domestic residence, and on the roadside the guard post is still in its original position. Across the road, the remains of the station's sewage works can be seen.

CH sites had a large staff. For example, in 1942 it is reported to have had a total complement of about 250 men and women. These would have been RAF and WAAF operations staff, with Army personnel manning the perimeter defences and anti-aircraft positions. It's not clear where all these people were accommodated, but it is believed that it was mainly further along the A696 at Raylees. There are a number of air raid shelters here, and what is thought to be the site's fire engine station, nearby.

RAF Craster

The site at Craster has two surviving buildings. The radar operations building itself has four columns built into the walls. These were to take the weight of the aerial gantry which was on the roof. A hole in the roof was for the shaft which rotated the aerial. The second building housed a generator set which powered the site, the base of which can be seen.

The area around the Craster radar station has been investigated in detail by archaeologists and a large number of other wartime remains have been discovered relating to the defence of the site, including gun pits and mine fields There are even gardens created by Italian PoWs who were held there later in the war.

Radar building at Craster

Generator building at Craster

RAF Spittal

As with Craster, two buildings survive, the radar operations building and a generator house.

RAF Cresswell

The foundations of the earlier CHL site at Cresswell can be seen in the grass next to the road. This site suffered from relatively poor performance throughout its life due to its lower elevation. Most other similar sites were built on higher cliffs.

The later CHEL site was built further inland but there are no remains.

Foundations of the earlier CHL radar site at Cresswell

Anti-invasion Defences

Its island status has kept Britain free from any major foreign incursion since 1066. Despite this, invasion from the sea was a major national obsession. The Spanish, with their 1588 Armada and the French, during the Napoleonic period all created a climate of fear across the nation. Even during WW1, plans were put in place to evacuate coastal areas and create a sterile zone in case of German invasion. It is perhaps therefore a little surprising that up until the Dunkirk evacuation there had been very little anti-invasion planning for this current conflict.

Although Britain and France declared war on Nazi Germany in September 1939, little fighting took place in the west until May 1940, when the German forces advanced rapidly across the Low Countries, cornering the British Expeditionary Force at Dunkirk and other channel ports. The evacuation of nearly 340,00 soldiers from the Channel beaches was a success, but Britain was now faced with the immediate prospect of invasion. A massive construction programme was therefore initiated, building a range of defences across the country. That the vast majority of these defences were constructed in a period of less than four months is a staggering feat that must have involved a large part of the population and probably the majority of building contractors up and down the country. The amount of construction was so great that national shortages of concrete were being reported at times during 1940. What we can see today of the defences is made up mainly of concrete blocks on the beaches and pillboxes across the landscape. These pillboxes in particular can often seem to be randomly distributed, but a quick look at the map of the ones which survive shows the outline of the strategy that was being employed.

In May 1940, General Ironside was tasked with the job of putting in place the necessary anti-invasion defences. He immediately drew on the traditional strategy of that time which involved static defence lines. These were intended to slow down or halt the advancing enemy, while allowing reinforcements to be brought to bear at the required locations.

On the coast, this defence line strategy was known as Coastal Crust. The 'crust' was a continuous, but thin, line of defences along all vulnerable coastlines. Inland, a series of Stop Lines was laid out which made use of existing landscape features wherever possible, such as hills, rivers and canals. They were made up of pillboxes to provide strong points with newly constructed barriers such as anti-tank ditches. All of this was intended to slow, and hopefully halt, the

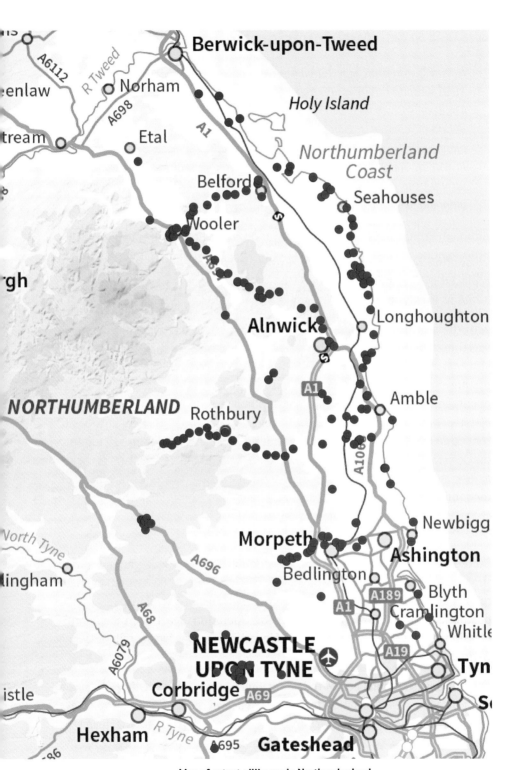

Map of extant pillboxes in Northumberland

advance of an invading force.

The main spine of this inland system was planned at a national level and was called the GHQ line. Local area commanders were given the task of augmenting this backbone, using their specific knowledge of the landscape. It was partly by such delegation that so much was built in such a short time. It was recognised that not all of these inland lines could be fully manned, the plan being instead to occupy positions as necessary to counter the specific invasion threat that might emerge.

The stop-line strategy was, however, starting to raise some criticism at a national level due to its essentially static nature. The stop lines were extremely difficult to man as they often were in isolated areas, and once breached or bypassed, the whole line would become effectively useless. By mid-July, Ironside had been replaced by General Brook (later to be Lord Alanbrook), who reconfigured the strategy. Newly returned from France, he was able to bring in his first-hand experiences from the Battle of France where he had seen how the Blitzkrieg tactics relied on the rapid movement of troops, mainly along existing roads rather than across open land.

His new strategy, while retaining the coastal crust, focused on restricting any enemy advances by holding 'nodal points', such as towns, villages and crossroads. The defence lines were, where possible, adapted to meet this new plan, with more pillboxes and roadblocks being built around and within key towns. Much of the actual manning of these defences was gradually transferred to the newly established Home Guard battalions, who could now operate within their own town or village, releasing the Regular Army for other duties, including being ready to reinforce the area where an invasion had actually occurred, as well as operations overseas.

During all of this construction work the Battle of Britain was being fought in the skies of southern England. We now know that the failure of the Luftwaffe to achieve air superiority over the intended invasion beaches led to the postponement and then cancellation of Operation Sea Lion, the planned invasion of Britain. In 1941, the threat of invasion here was further reduced when Germany invaded Russia.

The anti-invasion defences were kept active, however, as it was felt that there was a strong possibility that Russia could have been defeated which would have probably resulted in Britain again coming under invasion threat. It is also possible that the government saw these anti-invasion activities as helping to keep the nation focused on the war, providing a daily reminder of the serious situation the nation was in, at a time when the Allies were not able to strongly engage with the enemy elsewhere.

Anti-tank blocks at the Holy Island causeway

Sandbag type gun position at Alnmouth

Coastal Crust

With its wide sandy beaches, Northumberland was seen as a prime invasion target, particularly for a diversionary force from Nazi occupied Norway. As a result, this whole area became a vast defended zone, with public access to the coast being prohibited. Most conspicuous, of course, are the concrete anti-tank cubes which can be seen on almost all the county's beaches though, over time, many have been buried by the shifting sands, moved by the actions of the sea and deliberately relocated to create new defences against coastal erosion. These blocks were cast in situ and were normally laid out in double rows with barbed wire strung between them.

Between the blocks, small gun posts were built, often using concrete filled sandbags. Time has not been kind to these defences, and most can now only be seen as piles of rounded concrete blocks, though after winter storms, some less damaged examples may be revealed.

There are a couple of great examples of how all of this would have looked in 1940, at the Lindisfarne causeway and at Cheswick. At these locations everything has been protected from the worst effects of nature and you can see the concrete blocks in rows, remnants of the barbed wire fastenings on the blocks and well-preserved machine-gun posts.

The shoreline was strewn with layers of barbed wire and scaffolding was erected below the high tide line to deter landing craft. Little remains of these defences

Gun position within the coastal defences at Cheswick

Anti-glider poles near Holy Island

though some scraps do appear from time to time as storms move the sand dunes.

The risk of invasion by glider-borne troops was understood and a series of anti-glider defences were constructed in order to deter landings. On some of the larger beaches old cars were filled with stones and staked to the sand below the high-water line. Though most of these have been removed or have corroded away, remnants can sometimes be found at Bamburgh and Beadnell, particularly after heavy storms.

In other areas, such as the mud flats to the north of the Lindisfarne causeway, anti-glider poles were erected. Remarkably, some of these have remained in position. Also anti-glider and anti-tank ditches were dug near the coast, and although these have in the main been filled in there are still some surviving at Druridge Bay.

The coastal defences were completed with a series of pillboxes and gun emplacements built close to the shore. Pillboxes can be found all along the coast; they are particularly plentiful in the area around Embleton Bay and Craster. Gun emplacements housed larger guns and were usually built at the ends of beaches where they could provide enfilading fire along the shoreline.

Good examples of such emplacements survive at Cocklawburn and Budle Bay. Some are quite dilapidated like the collapsed emplacement found at the base of the cliff near Longhoughton. Others are almost completely buried in sand, as

Anti-tank ditch at Druridge Bay

Lozenge pillbox at Druridge Bay

Pillbox built on top of an earlier 19th century gun emplacement at Alnmouth

at Birling Carrs near Warkworth.

There are also the remains of a number of gun emplacements along the coast to the north of Newbiggin-by-the-Sea, with a particularly impressive set of pillbox defences near Lynemouth power station.

Many of these emplacements housed old naval guns, which had been put into storage when warships were scrapped, as more modern weapons were still in short supply. There are even stories of telegraph poles being used as imitation gun barrels in order to deceive enemy reconnaissance flights.

Finally, though not strictly 'coastal crust', the WW1-era gun battery at Blyth was

Gun emplacement at Cocklawburn

Gun emplacement near Beacon Point

brought back into operation. Blyth was Northumberland's most important port during the war (and during the Great War as well), from where the coal from the nearby mines was shipped around the country. We should remember how important coastal shipping was at this time – there was not the scale of road transport that we see today. There was also an important submarine base, HMS Elfin. The defence of the port was a high priority.

The site had originally been built during WW1 in the aftermath of the 1914 German naval bombardment of the east coast towns of Hartlepool, Whitby and Scarborough. Work had started in 1916, but was only completed in 1918, too late to have any active role in the war, and the site was subsequently disarmed and mothballed.

Blyth Battery

In February 1940 work started on recommissioning the site. The gun positions themselves were fitted with two new six-inch guns and a concrete roof was installed to provide protection to the gunners from air attack, a risk not existing during WW1.

A new Battery Observation Post (BOP) was built, housing modern ranging equipment. This can still be seen alongside the earlier BOP from WW1.

The combined WW1/ WW2 battery has been restored by local volunteers who hold regular open days. Recently, the gun emplacements have been fitted with replica guns. The external parts of the site are accessible all the time.

Inland Stop Lines

Northumberland's main inland defence lines made use of the Coquet and Wansbeck rivers as natural defences. The pillboxes in both lines were constructed to the south of the rivers and are generally well preserved. They were intended to eventually provide a defence line from the Cheviot Hills to the coast, where they would have linked to the 'coastal crust'. The Coquet Stop Line starts at the edge of the hills, near Hepple, with a pillbox every mile or so, though it does peter out near Felton. The Wansbeck Stop Line seems never to have extended further west than Meldon, perhaps a victim of the change in strategy

Lozenge pillbox in the ramparts of Old Bewick hillfort

in July 1940, while there is little to be seen east of Morpeth due to later developments and mining.

Supporting these main stop lines, two subsidiary lines were built to the north of the Coquet, between Wooler and Belford, and Wooler and Alnwick. These two lines have survived almost complete, though it has to be noted that these latter two lines do seem to be a little ill-conceived. As an example, the two pillboxes at Old Bewick hillfort, and the two others in the valley to the east can have provided little, if any, strategic defence. You could believe that the lines had been designed miles away by someone drawing a line on a map, taking no account of local conditions. We shouldn't be too critical of this, however, as the whole strategy was developed and implemented within a few weeks of the Dunkirk evacuation.

Nodal Point Defences

In Northumberland, nodal point defences were located mainly around the county's towns and villages. Most of these defences have subsequently been lost due to developments, but there are enough remains to make this an interesting point of exploration.

D pillbox at Eglingham

Morpeth was ringed with pillboxes. The ones to the south have been lost under post-war housing developments, but a number have survived to the north. Examples can be seen alongside the road between Mitford and Fairmoor.

Wooler still has at least seven pillboxes around its perimeter. Belford was similarly defended, though like Wooler, it is difficult to separate the 'nodal point' defences from the earlier 'stop lines'. The small village of Eglingham interestingly has pillboxes guarding three of the four roads that meet here. It is not known whether any defences previously existed on the fourth road. Alnwick has three beehive pillboxes on the north side of the town, adjacent to the river Aln.

As well as these town and village defences, isolated pillboxes can be seen at

Beehive pillbox on the River Aln near Alnwick

Loophole near Morpeth's Telford Bridge

Roadblock near St. Michael's church in Alnwick

strategic locations, such as on the north side of the (now demolished) railway bridge at Powburn.

As well as pillboxes, buildings and walls were adapted to provide defensive positions. At Morpeth there is a large gun embrasure on the south side of the Telford Bridge. Smaller loopholes can be seen at Bothal and Ulgham. Alnwick has a number of loopholes in the cemetery wall on the south side of the town, which would have covered the town's southern entrance. There are at least two other locations in the town where the remnants of loopholes can be seen; one is high on the wall of a building overlooking the Lion Bridge, with others in a wall on Canongate.

As well as pillboxes and loopholes, roadblocks were built in towns on the major through-roads. Most of these have been lost, but a number can still be seen if one knows what to look for. Roadblocks normally consisted of three staggered rows of deep sockets dug in the road into which, in the event of an invasion, would be fitted vertical steel rails. Such roadblocks can leave a distinctive mark in the form of rows of dimples in the road's surface, where, despite the best efforts of subsequent resurfacing works, the road continues to subside into the deep sockets that had been dug.

At Alnwick in particular the remains of at least five roadblocks can be seen – outside St Michael's Church, outside the Mechanics' Institute on Percy Street,

Grey Lane, at the junction of Prudhoe Street and Dovecote Lane and by the bridge over the old railway on Bridge Street. Two others, on South Road near the old railway station, were revealed during major roadworks but have now disappeared – for the time being at least!

The remains of roadblocks can also be seen at Rothbury, on the south side of the main bridge, and at Lucker, immediately next
to the level crossing.

Home Guard assembling a roadblock
[public domain]

A roadblock near the Lucker level crossing

The Auxiliary Units

This chapter is slightly different, in that there are no relics of the Auxiliary Units that can be easily seen in the landscape. Most have been destroyed, either by demolition or erosion. Of those that have survived, all are on private land, and by their very nature are hard to find. These survivors are so fragile now, that indiscriminate visiting should be discouraged, but hopefully, in the future, some of these might be restored and so preserved for the future. Nevertheless, the story of the Auxiliary Units is so interesting it seems appropriate to include it.

In the immediate aftermath of the Dunkirk evacuation, and alongside the massive construction programme that had been started to build fortifications across the country, men and women were recruited and trained for a dramatic last-ditch defence against the expected Nazi invasion. The Auxiliary Units (AU) were volunteers who, in the event of a successful enemy landing, were to stay behind enemy lines and carry out acts of sabotage and espionage in order to help the regular forces of the Army, Air Force and Navy push the invaders back into the sea. There is relatively little trace of the AUs in the landscape today, but the story is so dramatic that it is worth a separate chapter.

Plans to create such a clandestine force were being discussed for a number of years before the outbreak of war. The plans even developed to the point where secret supplies of explosives were hidden, mainly around South East England, to be used once the enemy had landed. The recruitment of the saboteurs didn't progress very far, however, but the ideas continued to develop, and by the middle of 1940 had started to take real shape. So much so, that when the ideas of Colonel John 'Jo' Holland of Military Intelligence were presented to the War Cabinet on the 1st July 1940, Churchill authorised immediate action and the Auxiliary Units were born.

A number of Regular Army Captains were appointed as field commanders with the title of Intelligence Officer (IO). Their job was to travel around the country and recruit suitable men to operate in six or seven man patrols from secret underground bases and in the event of an invasion, stay behind and attack enemy targets.

The IOs initially sought out likely patrol leaders, who would then be asked to name a number of men that they knew who could be completely relied upon.

The local Chief Constable was then asked for his input. Men known to drink heavily and to talk too freely would be excluded. This meant that the Chief Constable knew potentially every member of the local patrols, so his name was on an assassination list to guard their security. It could only be hoped that these senior policemen would have made themselves scarce once the invaders arrived!

The men who were selected tended to come from two main backgrounds; miners and quarry workers were seen as useful, because of their experience with explosives, while farm workers and gamekeepers (and poachers of course!) were sought for their knowledge of the land. These would also all be in reserved occupations (poachers apart of course) so allowing them to avoid being called up into the regular forces.

Each potential recruit would first be approached by the IO and asked if he was interested in serving his country in a potentially dangerous way. If the answer was "yes", then they had to sign the Official Secrets Act before further discussions could take place. Once this was done, the plan was explained and as far as is known, no-one backed off at this point. From the very beginning secrecy was paramount; it even went as far as not being able to tell their own families about what they would be doing.

Units were created at places all along the eastern and southern coasts of Britain, from Thurso in the North of Scotland to St David's in Wales, with 21 in Northumberland alone. Each Unit was made up of about four to six local men. They were given intensive training and provided with the most up-to-date weaponry and explosives. Sworn to secrecy, it is only relatively recently that families of those involved have discovered what their relatives had been committed to do.

The range of targets would have been very large. It would have included strategic bridges, roads, railways, RAF airfields that might be used by the Luftwaffe as well as German troop positions. It is also believed that the Auxiliaries were given a list of local people who would be assassinated, which could include known Nazi sympathisers and collaborators.

Initially, the Auxiliaries were not given a uniform, but it was realised that this stance would put them in real danger in the event of their capture. The lack of uniform would have placed them beyond the protection of the Geneva Convention which required combatants to be uniformed and have a clearly indicated chain of command.

The lack of uniforms had also began to cause problems locally, as people thought the patrol members were not doing anything to support the war effort. The Auxiliaries recalled this as being a most difficult period, with many locals "pointing their fingers at them", and there were even instances of them being sent a white feather. And despite this, they still maintained their silence.

The situation was resolved by the creation of a number of Auxiliary Battalions of the Home Guard. In all, three of these battalions were created. The official title of the local battalion was 201 Battalion GHQ Reserve Home Guard Auxiliary Units, which covered Scotland and Northumberland. Further south, 202 was for Durham to Essex and 203 from Kent to Cornwall.

The Auxiliaries were now given Home Guard uniforms, with special AU flashes. However, in all other respects besides the uniform, there was no contact with the Home Guard, though some patrol members had a dual role as members of the local Home Guard unit.

The scale of what they were being asked to do is hard to comprehend today. The behaviour of the Nazis in occupied Europe would have made it clear what would happen in Britain. The Auxiliaries, if caught, would have been subject to horrendous torture in order to try and extract information about other units, before being summarily executed. Also, the local population living in the occupied zone would have faced very real reprisals in the event of any attacks being carried out by the Auxiliaries against the occupying forces.

The range of weapons used by the Auxiliaries was varied. In the earliest days, they were issued with whatever became available, but later their equipment was more standardised, when they were often given items before specialised units such as the Commandos.

The first automatic rifle issued was the Browning (BAR), but this was not popular with the patrols as it was heavy and difficult to handle when moving fast through the countryside. This was superseded, initially by the Thompson and later by the Sten gun. Other firearms included the 0.22" sniper rifle and the ubiquitous Lee Enfield. Hand grenades, both explosive and smoke types, were also provided.

Most members of the Operational Patrols were issued with a personal 0.45" automatic pistol which they would keep at home. They were also each given a Fairbairn-Sykes knife, which would later became standard issue to the Commandos. With its 7-inch tapered blade, razor sharp edges and sharp point it was intended for use against sentries and others when silence was necessary.

The patrol members often produced their own silent weapons, such as the garrotte, made from a two foot length of piano wire with a wooden handle at each end, as well as brass knuckle dusters.

The patrols also had plastic explosive before it was issued to the Regular Army. A variety of pull, trip and pressure switches were all used to activate explosive booby-trap devices. They also had time pencil detonators, with the delay ranging from a few minutes to two weeks, though these were not always very accurate, particularly in cold weather; they could be anything from a few minutes to a couple of hours out. Latterly, the patrols used two pencils to improve the chances of an explosion being successful. The Auxiliaries used their ingenuity to solve specific problems. For example, cycle inner tubes filled with explosive, when placed on an aircraft wing root, quickly removed the aircraft's wings.

In the early days, the Operational Patrol leaders were sent to Coleshill House in Wiltshire for a weekend of intensive training in the use of explosives and the art of unarmed combat. The ample grounds were ideal for training purposes, while the large stable block was useful for the accommodation of the men. There was also an underground base, built to the design that would be used throughout the country.

Later, journeys to Coleshill were avoided due to the distance, which required the men to travel on a Thursday and not return till Monday. This aroused suspicion at work so, instead, training took place at 201 Battalion's HQ at Melville House, near Cupar in Fife.

Instructors were sometimes sent out to train the patrols and written instructions were also issued, with the patrols being left to practise whatever they were told to do. The Auxiliaries had their own "manual", which was printed to resemble an agricultural publication. There were two out-of-date calendars, followed by an old issue of The Countryman's Diary for 1939. Issued to all volunteers, their innocent titles covered a handbook on explosives, timing devices and suitable sabotage targets.

The skills developed by the Auxiliary Units were very much appreciated by the regular forces. A number of the Northumbrian patrols were selected to accompany the Royal Family to Balmoral and act as guards in case of a kidnap attempt by the Germans. The tours lasted six weeks.

Each unit was provided with an underground base called an Operational Base (OB). The very first ones were built by the Auxiliaries themselves, to no specific design. Very quickly, however, a standardised design was produced, with the OBs

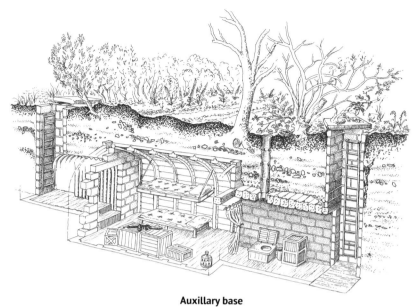

Auxillary base

Illustration by David Hopkins, by kind permission of Heritage Lincolnshire

being constructed by specialist units of the Royal Engineers. The standard design would be adapted to deal with local conditions, but the overall concepts were retained for most bases.

The construction work was done in total secrecy, often with searchlights or anti-aircraft guns brought in to provide the excuse for the creation of a restricted area while the OB was being built. Once the OB was complete, all signs of construction would be removed, leaving the base hopefully undetectable.

The standard OB was built underground and located adjacent to a stream, which would have provided a ready water supply, as well as a possible escape route. A large hole would be excavated, and a concrete floor created. The main chamber was semi-circular, about 9 metres long and 3 metres across. Formed from corrugated iron sections, similar to a Nissen hut, they were given the name "elephant shelters". At one end of this main chamber would be an entrance with a shaft leading to the surface. At the other end would be an escape tunnel which would exit at some distance from the OB. This was to provide an alternative exit route in case of discovery by the enemy. Both the entrance and the exit would be concealed by camouflaged trapdoors, operated by ingenious mechanisms. Once built, the whole structure was then reburied. The Auxiliaries were then left to build any fittings, such as tables and beds, themselves.

The inside of the OB was coated with a white paint that had small granules of coke incorporated into it. This was intended to absorb some of the excessive moisture that was produced by the men themselves, and by the stoves and candles that were used.

Close to the OB would be a separate observation post, which would be manned by a member of the unit. Linked to the main OB by telephone, the observer would be able to report any enemy activity in the immediate area.

As well as weapons, ammunition and explosives, a typical Operational Base would have had enough rations for about fourteen days, and in a sealed stone jar, a gallon of rum to be used only in an emergency.

As far as we know, all the main OBs in Northumberland were built by the 184th Tunnelling Division of the Royal Engineers, with most in use by the summer of 1942, and the last ones, in the north of the county, being complete before the end of that year.

At the end of the war, all signs of the AUs were supposed to have been destroyed, though most of the twenty one Operational Bases in Northumberland initially

Hebron Operational Base, with white water-absorbing coating

Collapsed Operational Base at Falloden

avoided this fate. But where explosives failed, time has taken its toll. After more than 75 years, they are all slowly deteriorating. Many have now collapsed, while some have been lost completely under new developments or by mining and quarrying. By their very nature the OBs are difficult to find, and all known surviving examples are on private land. Only a very few are recognisable for what they were, and even these will probably soon disappear.

In addition to the sabotage units of the Auxiliary Units, there was also an Auxiliary Unit established to gather intelligence about the deployment of enemy troops. As with the sabotage units, they were expected to work behind enemy lines, communicating intelligence back to the British forces in any unoccupied zone that might have survived. Known as the Special Duties Section (SDS), they operated totally separately from the Operational Patrols, with separate IOs. Later many IOs became responsible for both parts of the AUs, though the unit members remained unaware of each other's existence, even when operating in the same areas.

The official stance of the government was that, in the event of invasion, the general population should stay put rather than evacuate. The 'Keep Calm and Carry On' poster which was famously rediscovered at Barter Books in Alnwick, but was never actually used, was part of the programme of encouraging people not to leave their homes. This is in sharp contrast to the plans developed for WW1, where the population was to be evacuated from any invasion area, destroying anything left behind that might be useful to the enemy.

The Special Duties section consisted of three layers of recruit, all of whom must have been willing to stay behind after an invasion, while still being able to move relatively freely about the countryside. Firemen, farmers and vicars were particularly useful, though policemen were not recruited as it was anticipated that they would have been forced to cooperate with the Germans to keep law and order. Firstly, local people were trained in recognising troop formations and how to report these via a dead letter drop. These dead letter drops could include such locations as under a stone, in a hollowed-out gate hinge or under the number plate on a telegraph pole.

The messages would be collected by a 'runner' and delivered to the local Out Station, again by dead letter drop.

The Out Station, was a clandestine radio transmitter, operated by local people. They would then communicate to a Control Station, who would pass the information to the Army, who it was hoped would still be operating in the unoccupied parts of Britain. The only confirmed Out Station in Northumberland was within Longhorsley Tower, though this has since been lost.

The Control Station would be in an above-ground building, but once an invasion

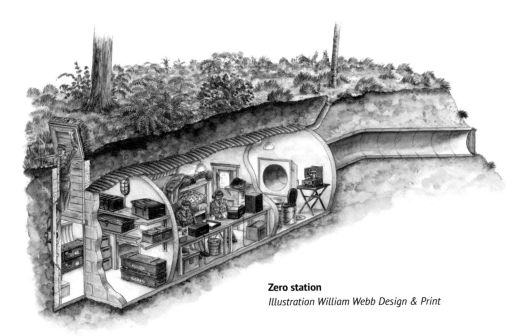

Zero station
Illustration William Webb Design & Print

was imminent, this would be abandoned, and the operators would move into an underground Zero Station which was constructed in an underground hide, similar to, but larger than that used by the sabotage Auxiliary Units – slightly longer as there is an extra chamber for the generating equipment necessary to keep the radio batteries charged.

There was one Zero Station in Northumberland, at Heiferlaw, to the north of Alnwick. This is on private land and not accessible to the public. Today, as the photographs in this book testify, the Heiferlaw Zero Station is probably the best preserved of all the Auxiliary Unit's underground facilities in Northumberland. As an SDS site, it might well have been built to a better standard, and being on higher ground, it has probably been saved by the drier conditions. It is now, together with its surrounding Iron Age enclosure, a scheduled monument. This of course only protects it from deliberate damage and doesn't provide any specific preservation.

The radio communication was all by spoken word, rather than Morse. A simple spoken code was used, where specific words such as tank, aircraft etc. were changed to another, more innocuous, word. The code sheet was changed daily. The Control and Zero Stations were operated by women from the Auxiliary Territorial Service (ATS).

The entrance to Heiferlaw Zero Station

Inside the Zero Station at Heiferlaw

The radios that were used by the Special Duties section were especially designed for the purpose. They operated on very high frequencies (VHF) between 48 and 60 megacycles, which it was believed were neither used nor monitored by the German forces. It was also thought that these VHF signals would only operate on 'line of sight'; the signals would not transmit over the horizon, which would reduce the chances of being detected.

In this way the aim was to make life very difficult for any invading force, and ultimately to be able to retake the initiative and so repel the enemy. Whether this would have been successful is now an academic question, but the very existence of the two parts of the Auxiliary Units demonstrated the lengths to which the anti-invasion preparations would go.

As we know, the invasion never came. The Battle of Britain was won in the skies by the young pilots of the RAF, and the Luftwaffe never achieved the air superiority necessary for a seaborne invasion. The plans for Operation Sea Lion were postponed in September 1940 and then cancelled for good.

In June 1941, Germany invaded Russia. Initially it seemed that Russia too would be conquered and so the invasion threat remained. By the end of 1942, however, German forces were bogged down on the Eastern Front, and would soon start to retreat. Together with the Allied victory at El Alamein in November of that year, it marked the turning point.

Despite it being clear that any German invasion was now out of the question, the Auxiliaries were maintained in an operational state through to 1944, perhaps in order to keep them in readiness for things to come.

The SDS were stood down in July 1944. There was no formal recognition of their role; they had to be content with letters from their commanding officers which ended as follows:

> "As no public recognition can be given for this job, so well done, it is my wish that a copy of this letter be sent to all members of the Special Duties Organisation as my own acknowledgement of the value and efficiency of their work."

In the run-up to D-Day, some of the Northumberland patrols were sent to the Isle of Wight as there was a fear the Germans might detect the invasion plans and launch an attack there in order to disrupt the embarkation.

The Operational Branch were finally stood down a little later, in November 1944. Again there would be no official recognition apart from a letter. Some of the Auxiliaries went on to volunteer for service with the Special Operations Executive (SOE) and the Special Air Service (SAS).

At the end of the war, anyone who served in the war in a non-military capacity was given the Defence Medal. The Auxiliaries received no such recognition.

The existence of the Auxiliary Units was never made public. The SDS radios were all collected and destroyed; no example exists today, though there have been efforts to build replicas. All the OBs were closed down, and some were destroyed. The equipment was recovered though much of the explosive seems to have been 'dispersed' and was used for years to come by farmers for clearing tree stumps! The jars of rum were all collected, but unsurprisingly many patrols found ways of getting to the rum without breaking the seal!

To the end, most of the Auxiliaries kept their silence. Some did eventually talk about their experiences, from whom we have most of our knowledge of what happened during those times of desperate need.

Firing butt at RAF Morpeth

Blister hangar at RAF Morpeth

Training Airfields

As the immediate threat of invasion diminished, and with the arrival of American forces in the UK, plans turned to thoughts of the liberation of Europe. In Yorkshire, there was a major expansion in Bomber Command airfields, while all across East Anglia, many American airbases were built. As well as these operational airfields, many new bases were built for the training of the aircrew required to support the growing air war. The construction programme was immense. By 1945 there were over 700 airfields in the UK. Northumberland's open skies, away from the more congested areas further south, made it an ideal area for training facilities and five new airfields were opened in the county.

The airfields that were constructed from late 1941 were designated as temporary, only being intended to operate for the duration of the war. Their design followed a standard template, with adjustments to deal with local circumstances. There were usually three hard runways (concrete or tarmac) in a triangle arrangement to give the pilots the best chance of being able to land and take off into the wind. A perimeter track encircled the runways, linking a large number of circular dispersal points which were used to keep parked aircraft well separated to prevent them being an easy target for attackers. There was a wide range of support buildings for the airfield, including accommodation, administration, medical, stores and maintenance, which were dispersed in small groups in order to minimise casualties should an attack be carried out. These buildings were much simpler than the pre-war types, being steel framed, single-skin brick or prefabricated, such as the ubiquitous Nissen hut.

RAF Morpeth

RAF Morpeth was opened in early 1942 as an Air Gunnery School, training bomber air gunners. A seven-man Lancaster crew, for example, would include three air gunners, one of whom had the main role of bomb-aimer. The expanding Bomber Command campaign, and the heavy losses suffered by the bomber crews, required a steady flow of trained gunners.

The gunners would initially be trained on the ground using turrets mounted on rails in order to create the sense of movement required to master the skill of air to air firing. The remains of two large brick-built firing butts which would have been used for this are still in place.

Later, the trainees would progress to live firing against aerial targets, using the offshore ranges, such as at Druridge Bay. The gunners would use aircraft types such as the Avro Anson, which was equipped with a single powered turret, with targets being towed by Westland Lysanders and Miles Martinets.

Though most of the airfield's structures have been demolished, sections of the runways and taxiways are still in place, and a public footpath allows parts of these to be walked. Of particular interest is the large blister hangar that is still in use as a store for a local farm. Such hangars would have been common on the airfields in the county.

The woods surrounding the old airfield contain the remains of buildings, including air raid shelters and blast trenches, which, due to their robust construction, have survived.

Blast shelter at RAF Morpeth

RAF Milfield

RAF Milfield, opened in early 1942, was built on the site of the Woodbridge WW1 landing field. This airfield was used for training pilots in ground attack, mainly using Typhoon and Tempest aircraft. Training for these types of operations proved to be very important as they would be used in supporting troops on the ground in the days following D-Day. It was very dangerous, involving low flying at very high speeds.

Much of this airfield has been lost due to sand extraction in the area, though the northern end of the runway is still in existence, and parts of the perimeter track can be seen from the minor road which runs along the eastern side. Indeed, part of the road to the east of the airfield uses the old perimeter track.

There were a number of dispersed sites, in particular for accommodation. These were in what are today woodlands to the south and west. Few buildings remain, though a Machine Gun and Cannon range is still surviving in the fields to the east of the airfield site.

Today the airfield site is used for gliding, and there is a memorial to the pilots

Firing butt at RAF Milfield

Memorial at Maelmin

TO HONOUR THE MEN AND
WOMEN THAT SERVED AT
RAF MILFIELD FROM 1941-1946
AND TO THOSE THAT LOST
THEIR LIVES AT THIS FACILITY

who trained here outside the modern club house. There is a second memorial near to the Maelmin heritage site.

There was a decoy site for Milfield at Lowick but its exact location is not currently known.

The training at Milfield made much use of a series of live firing ranges. The beaches at Cheswick and Goswick were used for target practice, with the area being littered with various targets such as old vehicles, tanks and even railway locomotives. There are rumours that one of the dunes on the beach is formed from the remains of these targets. Vast quantities of live ordnance were fired here and until as recently as 2012, a team of RAF bomb disposal experts was based on the beach, carrying out regular clearances and controlled explosions.

Of the range itself, two range towers survive on the beach area, with one being built on top of an anti-invasion pillbox, a demonstration of the shift from the defence of the early war years to that of offence.

Inland, Doddington Moor and Horton Moor, were used as ground attack ranges. These ranges were only a few minutes flying time from the airfield at Milfield, which meant that the aircraft would be attacking their targets immediately after take-off. This turned out to be the situation that the pilots would encounter in action after D-day, where they were often operating from bases just behind the front line.

Range tower and pillbox at Cheswick

RAF Brunton from the air

Air-raid shelter at RAF Brunton

RAF Brunton

RAF Brunton was opened mid-1942 as a satellite to Milfield in order to accommodate the large numbers of aircraft that were needed for the training there. Brunton has been largely untouched and is, together with Eshott, one of the most complete WW2 airfields in the county. In the past, many local teenagers were taken here to start driving, safely away from the roads, and a detachment from RAF Boulmer was based here for a period. Today, unfortunately, access to the site is very limited. A public right of way crosses the end of one runway, but the best views are probably from the adjacent road bridge over the railway where a number of airfield shelters can be seen.

Nearby are the remains of a HF/DF Direction Finding tower which was used to direct aircraft back to base.

There was a decoy site for Brunton at Elford, but its exact location is currently unknown.

RAF Eshott

RAF Eshott was conceived when, in 1941, some land to the south of Felton was acquired by the Air Ministry for the construction of a new airfield. It was originally intended to be a Fighter Command base, operating together with the other local base at Acklington. Construction started in early 1942, with three runways being built in the normal 'A' configuration of the period. The main runway's length was about 2000 yards, typical for an operational base, but longer than the training

Runway at RAF Eshott

Ablutions block at RAF Eshott

airfields built elsewhere in the county. The support buildings, were laid out in a number of separate sites to the south of the airfield.

Towards the end of 1942, before completion, the airfield was reallocated to 57 Operational Training Unit (OTU), a unit which trained new pilots to fly Spitfires. This was a single seat aircraft; only a very few two-seat versions were built. New pilots therefore had to take a leap into the unknown when they first took to the air in these high-performance machines, after very little flying training on more simple aircraft types.

At the airfield itself the runways are visible and many of the wartime accommodation buildings can be seen, particularly along the road down to Eshott Heugh. Parts of the perimeter track are still in use as roadways and some of the dispersal pads, where aircraft would be parked, can be seen. The sick quarters site can be seen adjacent to the farm at Helm. The airfield remains in use for private aircraft and microlights, utilising part of the old wartime runway.

Sick quarters at RAF Eshott

Buildings at RAF Boulmer

RAF Boulmer

In 1943, the final Northumberland airfield was opened at RAF Boulmer. This site, initially a decoy site for Acklington, was developed into a full airfield as a satellite for RAF Eshott. It was used for the advanced elements of the Spitfire pilot training programme, including air-to-air firing practice, using the nearby coastal ranges.

The airfield stayed in operation after the war, eventually hosting the Air Sea Rescue helicopters of 202 Squadron until 2015, when the service was civilianised.

The runway has long since been dug up, but its location can still be traced in the fields. Most of the site remains in operation with the RAF, but a few of the wartime era buildings can be seen near to the entrance of the modern Administration site

Remains of the runway at RAF Boulmer

Gloucester Lodge Heavy Anti-aircraft gun site

Searchlight base at Hadston

Other Sites

There are a small number of WW2 sites which don't readily fall into any of the main categories but are nevertheless worthy of description. These are therefore recorded here, in no particular order.

Anti-aircraft Guns

Blyth, as a key coal port, was protected by three heavy anti-aircraft gun positions. Of these only one remains, though it is remarkably complete. This battery is at Gloucester Lodge to the south of the town. During WW2 it had four 3.7 inch guns. The site remained operational for the first years of the Cold War. A lot of the buildings that can be seen today are from that later period. The site itself is on private land but much can be seen from the adjacent road, including the gun emplacements and the foundations of the barracks for the gun crew.

Searchlights

The air defences were well supported by searchlight positions which were able to illuminate night raiders and so assist both anti-aircraft gunners and fighter pilots. Little sign of most of these remains though the concrete base of one such site is on the beach at Hadston.

Other searchlight positions are often identified by the existence of a solitary FW3/22 pillbox which would have been used to provide the operators with protection from any air attack.

Type 22 pillbox at a searchlight site

High Frequency Direction Finding

Until the advent of improved radar systems, many Allied aircraft crashed after becoming disorientated. This confusion could be due to a number of reasons, including navigational errors, damage to navigation equipment or deliberate confusion caused by German radio operators. The loss of aircrew was a serious problem. One solution that was devised was High Frequency Direction Finding (HF/DF) or 'huffduff'.

The system was straightforward. An aircraft in distress would transmit a signal on a specific frequency. Specialised detection sites would determine the direction of the signal, with the results from two or more HF/DF stations being triangulated to give a firm location which could then be transmitted back to the aircraft.

One type of receiver comprised a three-storey wooden tower – wood being used to avoid electro-magnetic interference – surrounded by a brick enclosure which would protect the tower against blast from bombs. The wooden towers have long since been dismantled but a number of the brick enclosures survive.

The site at Shoreswood is publicly accessible and there are a number of explanatory information panels. Another site can be found at RAF Brunton.

HF/DF was later replaced by a VHF system. At least three of these sites have survived, one at RAF Acklington and two at RAF Ouston.

Ross Anti-tank Range

The coast near Ross was used as an artillery range for anti-tank gunnery practice. Opened in 1942, the site included a narrow-gauge railway system on which self-propelled wagons could move. The wagons had canvas targets mounted on top so providing a moving target for the gunners. The track layout consisted of four main interconnected loops which are visible on aerial photographs.

The building which housed the wagons is still in use by the farm and can be seen from the public footpath that runs through the dunes to the sea. One of the four structures which would have been used by the range staff to repair holes in the canvas targets as firing was ongoing can also be seen nearby. No public access is allowed to the site, apart from the public footpath.

The Ross facility was closed in 1956 and relocated to Silloans on the Otterburn ranges.

HF/DF site at Shoreswood

Range bunker at Ross Sands

Featherstone PoW camp

Featherstone PoW Camp

As the war proceeded, and Allied successes grew, there were increasing numbers of prisoners of war to be held. Initially these were Italian, mainly from the North Africa campaign, who were generally treated with a high degree of freedom, often working on local farms during the day. Later, the prisoners would be German. Camps were created across the country, as well as overseas, in Canada for example. There were at least eight camps in Northumberland alone.

Nationally, most of the camps have been dismantled, though a few have survived. Eden Camp in Yorkshire, now a museum, is a notable survivor. In Northumberland, there are significant remains of Camp 18, which was built in the grounds of Featherstone Castle near Hexham. Originally constructed as a training base for American soldiers in the run up to D-day, it was later used to house German prisoners. It was one of the larger camps in the country, with 200 huts and space for 4,000 officers and 600 orderlies.

German prisoners were screened to determine their sympathies and divided into three groups; low risk anti-Nazi, medium risk and high risk hard-line Nazis. Camp 18 was used to house hard-line prisoners, which included a broad range of men from the German armed forces, as well as diplomats and bureaucrats. The camp

Bases of huts at Featherstone PoW camp

ran a 'denazification' programme to re-educate the prisoners prior to their return to Germany. The training was deemed a success and as time progressed, the prisoners were given increasing freedom to work in the local community.

On 1st April 1945, eight prisoners escaped. One unfortunately drowned, attempting to cross the flooded Tyne, while the other seven were quickly recaptured near Alston.

Two buildings can still be seen on the site of the camp, as can the foundations of prisoners' huts.

Gazetteer

RAF Fighter Command Airfields

Ashington WW1 Airfield

Bomb store	NZ 2446 8846

RAF Acklington

Airfield	NU 23 00
Pillboxes	NU 2241 0119, NU 2220 0069, NU 2393 0036, NZ 2333 9987
VHF station	NU 2346 0222
Q' decoy	NZ 2624 9434

RAF Ouston

Airfield	NZ 08 70
Pillboxes	NZ 0694 6992, NZ 0697 6901, NZ 0801 6849, NZ 0767 6872, NZ 0765 6874, NZ 0759 6851, NZ 0755 6956, NZ 079 705, NZ 0884 7037, NZ 0749 6875, NZ 0901 7046
Fire trenches	NZ 0760 6867, NZ 0759 6864, NZ 0760 6853
VHF Stations	NZ 0706 7041, NZ 0770 6868
'Q' Decoy	NZ 1763 7575

Radar

Fulwell sound mirror	NZ 3906 5967

Ottercops Moss

Type 22 pillboxes	NY 9409 8985, NY 9491 9007, NY 9549 8938, NY 9471 8854
Type 24 pillboxes	NY 9453 8920, NY 9424 8973, NY 9462 8968, NY 9456 8973, NY 9439 8988, NY 9513 8938, NY 9441 8933
Reserve stations	NY 9514 8948, NY 9438 8984

Other radar sites

Craster	NU 255 204
Spittal	NU 008 502
Cresswell	NZ 301 926

Anti-invasion Defences

Coastal Crust

Gun emplacements	NNU 253 078, NU 161 358, NU 032 481, NZ 314 895
Anti-tank trenches	NZ 275 966
Anti-glider poles	NU 085 443
Pillboxes	NU 052 463, NU 080 433, NU 130 368, NU 148 369, NU 179 355, NU 198 342, NU 234 290, NU 214 285, NU 234 254, NU 243 229, NU 246 225, NU 244 221, NU 253 223, NU 257 215, NU 248 213, NU 253 198, NU 261 145, NU 258 121, NU 251 111, NU 246 101, NU 251 063, NU 251 046, NU 258 004, NZ 275 967, NZ 314 895, NZ 320 799, NZ 335 768
Blyth Battery	NZ 320 793

Stop Lines

Wansbeck stop line	NZ 244 871, NZ 236 862, NZ 173 858, NZ 169 855, NZ 155 849, NZ 144 849, NZ 140 843, NZ 133 846
Coquet stop line	NU 244 046, NU 203 033, NZ 190 999, NZ 150 993, NZ 139 983, NZ 126 984, NZ 114 985, NZ 099 994, NZ 087 996, NU 068 004, NU 058 015, NU 046 010, NU 036 011, NU 022 016, NU 009 014, NU 001 007, NT 993 004, NY 985 998, NT 978 001, NT 973 000
Alnwick-Wooler stop line	NU 191 153, NU 188 164, NU 179 180, NU 162 180, NU 132 202, NU 119 199, NU 106 204, NU 091 209, NU 085 214, NU 076 216, NU 076 215, NU 063 227, NU 052 227, NU 045 245, NU 033 258, NU 019 263, NU 011 269
Belford-Wooler stop line	NU 104 351, NU 104 347, NU 104 346, NU 100 345, NU 093 341, NU 088 337, NU 073 332, NU 062 332, NU 047 322, NU 035 318, NU 016 315, NU 016 310, NU 012 304

Nodal point defences

Wooler	NT 983 278, NT 984 280, NU 006 286, NU 005 282, NT 984 275, NT 987 284, NT 989 285, NT 993 287, NT 989 276, NT 987 276
Alnwick	NU 200 136, NU 201 134, NU 206 130, NU 124 094
Morpeth	NZ 216 866, NZ 213 862, NZ 192 865, NZ 197 876, NZ 189 877, NZ 177 868, NZ 175 862

Training Airfields

RAF Eshott

Airfield	NZ 18 98

RAF Boulmer

Airfield	NU 25 13

RAF Milfield

Airfield	NT 95 33

RAF Brunton

Airfield	NU 20 25
HF/DF station	NU 198 254

RAF Morpeth

Airfield	NZ 17 82
Blister hangar	NZ 176 822
Firing butts	NZ 176 816, NZ 169 810

Other Sites

Gloucester Lodge HAA	NZ 320 785
Hadston searchlight base	NU 280 010
Searchlight sites (with type 22 pillboxes)	NZ 044 696, NZ 187 797, NZ 041 594
Shoreswood HF/DF	NT 936 463
Ross Anti-tank Range	NU 138 374
Featherstone PoW Camp	NY 674 603

Appendix 1 – **Pillbox Design**

Apart from the concrete anti-tank cubes, pillboxes are the most common wartime relic to be found in Northumberland with well over 200 examples surviving. There are a wide range of designs that have been employed, depending on the specific site being defended, the intended use of the pillbox and who actually built it.

Nationally a set of standard pillbox designs was developed by the Fortifications and Works Directorate of the War Department. Issued in the summer of 1940, these provided seven basic designs. These were given the designation FW3, followed by the specific type number, from 22 to 28, though each design type had many detailed variations making the specific type identification a bit of an art.

The FW3 designs are most commonly found at specific military sites such as airfields and radar stations. Such pillboxes would have been part of a high-level plan which is why it is likely that national standard designs would have been used. Construction of these major sites would have been by large contractors, familiar with military projects.

The details of the specific 'standard' pillboxes might vary. For example, thicker concrete might be used where greater strength was required. Wall thicknesses of about 12 inches were considered sufficient for protection against small arms, whereas 24 inches and more was deemed necessary for protection against heavier shells

Regionally developed defences usually used local designs, though why this was the case is unclear. These 'local' designs might be adaptations of national standards or may be unique to the specific area. Either way, their construction would normally have been by local, smaller, contractors.

This difference can be used to suggest what a pillbox's purpose would have been. Isolated pillboxes of the national FW3 standard were probably part of another facility, such as a searchlight or anti-aircraft gun position. Isolated pillboxes of local design are likely to be associated with stop lines or nodal point defences.

Concrete pillboxes are normally cast in situ, using some form of shuttering. Wood sheeting is the most common and the graining from this can often be seen imprinted in the concrete. Corrugated iron sheeting is also quite common, giving a distinctive wavy profile to the outer walls. Some concrete pillboxes have an

Type 22 pillbox, near Middle Duddo farm

outer layer of bricks which formed the shuttering.

Specific pillbox design features include the following, though not all designs incorporate all these features:

An internal anti-ricochet wall, designed to reduce casualties in the event of a bullet entering through an embrasure.

Stepped embrasures, to deflect bullets back outwards. These parts were often prefabricated parts. Earlier pillboxes often don't have this feature.

Internal shelves, usually in wood or concrete, for the rifleman to rest on, and to keep ammunition. Metal gun-support frames can also be found.

National Designs

Of the seven basic national designs, three can be commonly found in Northumberland.

FW3/22
The type 22 is a regular hexagonal pillbox. The wall and roof thickness can vary depending on its use. There will be an entrance on the rear face, normally with a porch, and there will normally be an embrasure on each face.

FW3/24
The type 24 is an irregular hexagonal design. Larger than a '22', it will generally have embrasures on each face and a rear entrance porch.

Type 24 pillbox, at RAF Ouston

FW3/26

The type 26 is the simplest of the standard designs, it is square and normally will have embrasures on two faces and no porch.

There are a small number of pre-fabricated pillboxes to this design which make use of standard concrete elements such as slotted posts and paving slabs, which are bolted together to create the final structure.

Pre-fabricated type 26 pillbox, near Dunstanburgh Castle

Local Designs

Lozenge

Of the local designs, the most common in Northumberland is the 'lozenge', a six-sided design, similar to a stretched type 22. It is only found in the North East of England. Some of these pillboxes have shaped concrete blocks nearby which were intended to reduce the size of an embrasure.

Lozenge pillbox near Mitford

Shaped concrete block for reducing the embrasure of a lozenge pillbox. This example is from Old Bewick hillfort.

D pillbox at Bothal Barns farm, near Ashington

D

This design is unique to Northumberland. It is a modified type 22, named the 'D' due to its plan shape.

Beehive

Made from concrete filled sandbags, this is the simplest pillbox design and could have been built with local labour and very limited machinery.

Beehive pillbox at Scroggs Hill, near Craster

Camouflaged Pillboxes

There are at least two examples of camouflaged pillboxes in the county, each of a unique design, they were intended to blend into the background.

Camouflaged pillbox at Druridge Bay

Camouflaged pillbox near Amble

Appendix 2 – **The Cold War**

The end of WW2 didn't bring the tranquillity that might have been hoped for. Very quickly the 'iron curtain' descended across Europe and the lines were drawn for what became known as the Cold War. It was a period defined by international tensions and the prospect of nuclear Armageddon. Much of what happened during this period was done in total secrecy and it is only with the collapse of the Soviet Union that some of Britain's secrets have been allowed to emerge. Many of us lived through this period oblivious to much of what was happening.

The threat of attack was coming from the USSR. Initially this was from Soviet bomber aircraft and later from their Intercontinental Ballistic Missiles (ICBM). The global strategy at this time was given the very apt acronym MAD (Mutually Assured Destruction) – both sides could more than destroy the whole world, so what purpose was there in attacking?

The Third World War didn't break out, though history shows us that this was a close call on more than one occasion! In the west, the stance was very much of

Russian map of Blyth

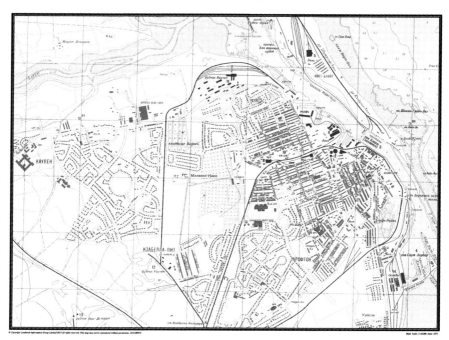

defence, providing sufficient show of force to deter an attack from the Soviet Union. The intent of the USSR became clearer when, after the fall of the Berlin Wall in 1989, plans of key British towns emerged with the labelling in Cyrillic script!

In the immediate post-war years, with the threat being primarily seen as bomber aircraft, many of the WW2 era heavy anti-aircraft gun sites were maintained and modernised. The site at Gloucester Lodge, near Blyth, was such an example. Indeed, most of what we see today is from this era, rather than WW2.

In order to be able to detect attacking aircraft the WW2 radar systems had to be improved and a new generation, called ROTOR, was developed. A number of sites were built along the east coast. At RAF Boulmer, ROTOR replaced the GCI set that had been relocated from Northstead. Over the years ROTOR was updated. Today, RAF Boulmer is the Control and Reporting Centre for the whole UK. There is no longer radar here; the local radar is now at RAF Brizlee Wood, to the west of Alnwick. This is one of just seven radar stations which provide total air defence cover for the whole of the UK and much of the surrounding seas – a major change from WW2, when Northumberland alone had eight radar stations!

As well as detecting a potential attack it was vital that any such threat could be rapidly and securely communicated through the NATO command structure. In a world before satellites such communication was not easy. Radio links relied on a clear line of sight between transmitting and receiving stations. Normal telephone lines were seen as being too vulnerable to disruption during a crisis.

In the late 1950s, a new system, known as Ace High, was developed which could transmit over very long distances by bouncing a signal off the troposphere layer of the atmosphere. The scattering of radio waves in this way was very inefficient and relied on both very powerful transmitters and very sensitive receivers to pick up the weak signals. The system was made to work, however, and it covered the entire NATO western boundary from Norway to Turkey. One of the 64 sites in this system was built at RAF Brizlee Wood. Ace High was eventually replaced by communication satellites.

Recognising the devastation that would be brought by a nuclear war, the British government sought ways to maintain some form of control of the surviving population. Reinforced bunkers were built where some form of government could be maintained after a nuclear attack. For the early period of the Cold War Northumberland was controlled from Catterick garrison but eventually in the 1970s a regional headquarters was established at Hexham. It was built within

Inside an ROC post

an old concrete WW2 cold store, a building which has now been demolished.

A new role was established for the Royal Observer Corps, with the job of spotting enemy aircraft now being redundant. Over 1500 underground posts were constructed throughout the country, normally very close to where their over ground observation posts had been. From here they could monitor the spread of the effects of a nuclear strike. The measurements that could be made included, for example, the direction and intensity of a nuclear blast and the residual radio-activity.

Teams of three or four members of the ROC would man these posts. In the event of an attack they would have had to remain underground for an extended period and so the posts had rudimentary accommodation, such as bunk beds and chemical toilets.

These ROC posts were built between 1957 and 1965 but were progressively decommissioned from 1968, with the final closures being in the early 1990s. The posts are all of a standard design and inside, many still have all their contents, as though they were just abandoned when shut down.

There were about 30 ROC posts in Northumberland, though only about half of these remain. One surviving example can be seen at Whittingham.

Due to the perceived vulnerability of the telephone network, a robust microwave communication system was created across the UK. This was made up of a network of radio stations and it was built and operated by the General Post Office. Its primary use was for Civil Defence but it also carried normal civilian communications. The most iconic of these radio stations is the Post Office Tower in London, but there is a spine of similar towers running up the country which is still in use today, though no longer for Civil Defence.

One of these radio stations was built in Northumberland, at Corby's Crag near Alnwick. Forming part of the main backbone, its design is much simpler than the towers that were used further south.

Whittingham ROC post

The entrance to an ROC post

Post Office mast at Corby Crags

Today we are used to having the satellite GPS system for navigation. In the days before this existed, long range navigational aids were still required when RAF aircraft needed to operate far from friendly bases. Dead reckoning navigation was used but was very inaccurate over long distances. During WW2 a number of systems were devised, including GEE. A GEE station was established at High Whittle near Shilbottle, but there are no traces remaining.

As the Cold War intensified, and NATO established its long-range bombing force, which included the RAFs 'V' bombers, an improved navigational system was required. The result was the LORAN (Long Range Navigation) system. The US Navy established a LORAN site at Low Newton, which operated from 1961 to 1978. The site is still there but is now used by the National Trust.

LORAN site at Newton-by-the-Sea

And last, but not least, the firing range at Druridge Bay was maintained until the mid-1950s, mainly being used by aircraft from RAF Acklington. A number of concrete building from this era remain.

Range building at Druridge Bay

Appendix 3 –
Stories from the Northumberland Auxiliaries

The following stories have been reproduced from the small book 'Most Secret', which is now out of print. Together, they provide a compelling and fascinating tale of the Northumbrian Auxiliary Units.

The first IO for Northumberland was Captain John "Hamish" Watt-Torrance. He was sent north to start organising the AU patrols. The first leader he recruited in Northumberland was Lambert Carmichael, a farmer from Scremerston. Lambert became, together with Joseph "Peter" Robinson and Les Riley, the core of the organisation in the north of the county. Their first meetings took place at a farm near Elford and at a safe house in Seahouses.

Lambert also proposed his brother, Alan, who farmed at Todburn, Longhorsley, who then went on to build the Longhorsley and Netherwitton patrols.

The first AU patrol in the county seems to have been established near Lambert's farm, early in 1941. Many of the unit's members were miners from Scremerston or farm hands and poachers with a good knowledge of the local countryside.

Their Operational Base was possibly at Inland Pastures Farm, with the entrance supposedly hidden in a cold frame, though this has not yet been confirmed. If true, it was probably created by the patrol themselves, prior to them getting a standard Royal Engineers' built base.

The patrols were organised into five regional groups which covered the whole county. The intention was that they could train together and share expertise. Once active, they could also operate as a larger force if the target required this.

Training was undertaken local to each patrol's area, where they would have practised the attacks they would be called upon to make after invasion. Sometimes a small practice area was set up, which may have been shared with a number of patrols. There was such an area near to the Allerdean patrol's OB which had a small arms training area with pop up targets.

Northumberland's Group 1, which comprised the three northernmost patrols also trained around The Island View Inn (ex Cat Inn) on the A1 near Scremerston, which they called the "Guerrilla Arms".

In early 1941, Captain Anthony Quayle (who would become a film actor, famous for his roles in *Ice Cold in Alex*, and *Guns of Navarone*) became the county's IO.

He was based at the Old Post Office in Chathill, which was conveniently situated next to the railway station.

He recounted a story to the Evening Chronicle in 1968. He had arranged an exercise for a Bedlington Patrol, where he would leave his staff car on a lonely road and the patrol of miners, led by banker Robert Hall, must regard it as a German tank. High on the moors, west of Morpeth, he told his driver to pull up by the side of the road. They stepped outside for a smoke to see how the patrol operated. Finally, with two hours gone and no sign of movement, he told the driver: "We've had enough - the miners must have been told to work an extra shift". He walked back to the car and opened the door.

Inside, a couple of them were smoking a cigarette, warm and comfortable. Another emerged from under the car and said he had planted the bomb. Then the rest of them rose from the roadside with guns pointed at me. Those chaps had been watching me for two hours - ever since we arrived.

He went on to add

> "One of the most amazing things I learned in Northumberland was just how valuable darkness was in this type of warfare. We taught the men that darkness was their friend and the axiom was constantly proved correct in exercises with regular troops."

The benefit of darkness is further demonstrated by the account of Tommy Wood, of the Longhorsley patrol, who recounted two 'exercises' he was involved in that further illustrated the skills of the Auxiliaries.

On one occasion, they were issued with a quantity of magnets covered in yellow paint, given instructions to go to Netherwitton, get inside the army camp, and place the magnets on the rear axles of any vehicles that were there. After doing this, they also left a few time delay 'bangers' and retired to the Institute Hall in the village.

All this was in the small hours and they were debriefing on the success or otherwise when they heard their time delay 'bangers' go off. It was shortly after that the Commanding Officer (CO) of the Netherwitton camp burst in demanding to speak to the person in charge of these "idiots". He claimed that he should have been notified in advance of any exercise involving his unit, because "my guards were armed you could have been killed." He was advised that to be realistic the exercise needed to be covert. The CO was not amused, especially when he was told that they had placed the magnets on all the rear axles of his unit's vehicles. The CO stormed out, after being told to check the metal beds where his men were sleeping, where he would find some more.

A similar exercise was carried out at Acton Hall, near Felton, where a Scottish Regiment of the 51st Highland Division was billeted. This time the Auxiliaries were well away before the subterfuge was disclosed to the Scots.

Further north, Captain Quayle, witnessed an exercise involving the Belford patrol and another unit of the 51st Division. Quayle hid himself in a laurel bush and waited for the action. As the bangers went off the Guard Sergeant could be heard shouting. "Shoot on sight and ask questions later". He waited until the furore had all died down, then quietly slipped away into the night, having witnessed another successful exercise carried out by his men.

Captain Quayle moved on to work within SOE in November 1941. He was replaced by Captain Victor Gough, who was in Northumberland until 1943, but was later killed by the Gestapo after being captured behind enemy lines in France. The final IO for Northumberland was Captain John Thouron.

Very little is known about the local Out Stations but we do know of one located in Longhorsley Tower. Bill Ricalton recalls

> "One of my friends, Pat Webb lived in the Tower with his parents. Pat was convinced that there was something hidden in their garage. We made several attempts, whenever the opportunity became available, to solve the perceived mystery — we found nothing. What had sown the seed of intrigue? Well, Pat had seen, on a number of occasions the Reverend Father Wright, a man of small stature who lived next door, going into their garage carrying a small milking stool. Answers from his parents, to his questioning, were always a vague inconclusive, "Well you know what Father is like.""

The truth only came out years later. The Tower was home to an Out Station. Access was gained by moving a shelf, which exposed a latch that opened a concealed panel. This gave access into the radio station. The aerial was believed to be hidden under the bark of a nearby tree.

The operators were Charles Webb, a solicitor who was the Master Observer in charge of the Longhorsley Observer Post and the Rev. Father Wright, who was an Air Raid Warden. He needed the milking stool to enable him to reach the catch, which opened the access to the radio room.

There is another story about an out station near Berwick. A farmer had his radio hidden in a shed behind a false wall. All went well for a time, until one night his little nephew, who was living with him, heard voices coming from the wall.

He ran and told his mother, who passed on the information to the military at a camp nearby. Within a short time, military personnel and Police pounced upon the farm, tore open a wall, and found the farmer crouched over the set.

He was immediately arrested and taken into custody. Naturally he dared not say anything as he was sworn to secrecy.

It took many hours for the farmer's leader to get him released; at that time, even the Chief Constable did not know anything about the organisation, so he had to get in touch with Whitehall. Later the Police Chiefs were notified, to prevent a repetition.

The recruitment into the Special Duties Section of the ATS provides an interesting window on the society of the day. Janet Wise (nee Purves-Smith), who eventually would operate the radios in the Alnwick area, recalled:

> "There was a Lady Claude-Hamilton who lived near here [Rusper in Sussex] and my father was Rector of this place. We were all, sort of, "jolly girls" in the area. It was very much that they wanted girls, who I don't think were wildly intelligent but more girls who they could be quite sure of their integrity. We were guaranteed a direct commission in this thing. Because they felt, because of this secrecy I mean, when we were manning a Station only three of us, and if we hadn't got commissions, how could we stop officers wanting to come in and "enquire"? But, with commissions, we could do just that. At that time, 1941, everybody felt that they must do something, and me and my sister, and various other girls around here were wondering what we wanted to do and we rather liked the idea of the WRENs because they had such beautiful uniforms! We thought the ATS were ghastly because they had such hideous uniforms! And then this Lady Claude-Hamilton, who lived up at Colgate, said to my mother: "You know. I could get your girls a direct commission in a frightfully interesting unit!" So, the thought of going into a terribly interesting unit, sort of outbalanced the horror of the uniform. Then we were told, when we said we were interested - two or three of my friends round here, me and my sister - we had to go up to somewhere in Essex and there was a Major Hill there, at that time, and we had to go for a voice-test. I think they were just looking us over though, actually but anyway we "Squawked" into this thing and then they said we were suitable applicants. Then I went to Halstead as an other-rank for about six-weeks, and then up to the OCTU [Officer Cadet Training Unit] at Edinburgh. And then one was

appointed. I was appointed down to Knepp Castle [West Sussex] which was the Divisional Headquarters of one of the Canadian Divisions at the time. From Knepp Castle we had our Out-Stations. What I think was quite clever was, there was no question, we knew their voices. We didn't know where they were; all we knew was that it was Harston One, Harston Two and Harston Three, which were the Out-Stations. It would be: "Hello Harston - Harston Two calling". And you knew it was him, so had a German had got into it or anybody else, one would have recognised the voice absolutely. But we didn't know who they were; we didn't know where they were, or anything about them. We had two sides. We were the Auxiliary Units Signals and then, in a "hushed breath" they were "the other side" which one didn't know about at all, except that there was this great cloud of secrecy that surrounded them. They were the operations side of things. The saboteurs and the chaps who went off into Europe, a lot of them with the SAS."

Sheila Trevaskis (nee Harrington) told a similar story. She joined the ATS in December 1942. After training she was selected for what was described as a "special and possibly dangerous" assignment. She was given a password and told to meet an ATS major, Beatrice Temple, niece of the then Archbishop of Canterbury, in Harrods, where she was interviewed over tea. Accepted into the Special Duties Section of the Auxiliary Units, she received training at the MI6 signals training school and later Coleshill House, before being posted to Alnwick.

Janet Wise, one of the Alnwick ATS operators, later remembered

"I was posted to Alnwick, in private "lodgings" for a while. Then we were sent off to Doxford Hall, which was the house of Lord Runciman. Our station in Alnwick was, I think, extremely good. We were right up on a hill about five miles outside of Alnwick on the site of some old Roman castle. A part of the old Roman wall was the entrance to our Zero Station. What happened was, that one pressed something in the wall and it just sort of came out and down we went, thirty-feet or so, to what we hoped looked just like an underground petrol store. It was a small area which was lined with these shelves all stacked with this petrol. Then you pressed something and one of these things just swung-out and then you had two chambers behind.

Our ordinary [Control] Station above ground was a Nissen-type hut and we would have to take our radios down below with us when we went to the Zero-Station which was about one hundred yards away.

We had one of these chambers which was big enough for two beds, a table and cupboard, and then you had these enormous felted-doors which closed through to where the sort of Elsan thing was and the charging-engine - I used to think it was rather like "Peter Pan", you know, all sorts of little tiny vents going on up to the surface you couldn't see. But when you put the charging-engine on, the doors were completely closed and these vents came into their full use and got rid of the exhaust fumes. We weren't [on air all the time], we had ten minutes exactly - ten minutes from the hour to ten-past and from the half-hour to twenty-to. So the men would always know that's when they could get us. Because, I mean, for secrecy's sake you don't want to be on the air for longer than you have to. So, that was our watch and that was when they could contact us."

Another of the Alnwick ATS operators, Dorothy Rainey (nee Monck-Mason), remembered

"The ATS subalterns lived in some style on booty from Lord Runciman's market garden, and from his gamekeeper and butler. Other delicacies appeared unexpectedly. We wrote up practice messages and coded them for the outstations to work out, and they did the same.

I talked to one jolly chap and he sent a message through - did I like salmon? I replied - of course - and he told me in code that he would put one on the train from Berwick and I could pick it up at Alnwick. Which I did, and we had a wonderful feast at Doxford Hall. Sometime later in a Berwick haberdashers, an upstanding chap came to serve me. I recognised the voice and later found out that he had caught the salmon himself on the River Tweed."

It is a pity that there are so few such stories from the Special Duties section.

It is perhaps fitting, however, to end with the words of Captain Anthony Quayle, who was interviewed in 1968 about his time with the Northumberland Auxiliaries.

"I remember with a great deal of affection the men and the people of the North-East. It was a wonderful place and I always felt very much at home there. I have a very warm feeling for the North-East - a rugged place with rugged, hardy people. A place with space to move and breathe."

Appendix 4 – **The Story of RAF Eshott**

The following information has been extracted, in the main, from the Operations Record Book for 57 OTU, which was based at RAF Eshott from early 1943 until the end of the war. The story is typical for the many airfields that were constructed during this period.

57 OTU was a Spitfire training unit. Up until the end of 1942, it was based at RAF Hawarden near Chester, but towards the end of that year it was forced to relocate as its airfield was being transferred to another training unit. 57 OTU needed a new base and the nearly completed RAF Eshott was one of the few available. So when the decision was taken to relocate 57 OTU, they were able to move to an almost completed airfield at Eshott, with a satellite airfield at Boulmer well on the way to completion.

The Movement Order was signed on 31st October 1942 and almost immediately the relocation started. On 3rd November, an advance party of WAAFs arrived by train. Due to women's quarters not being completed, part of the nearby Eshott Hall was requisitioned to provide accommodation for the 50 WAAF Other Ranks - they would be here until October 1943.

Training course 40, which had started at Hawarden in September 1942 had just finished so its 29 new pilots were sent out to operational squadrons. The partly completed course 41 was split, with some pupils going to other OTUs and the remainder transferring to Eshott along with course 42, though the pilots of 41 would only be at their new home for a short while, passing out on 15th December.

The main body of the training unit started to move northwards on three special trains and the OTU's aircraft were flown up, without incident. The first arrivals found an airfield only partly completed. Quarters were spread over five different sites and other separate sites had been built for communal activities, instruction and sick quarters.

The wartime plans show three large 100 foot span T1 hangars as well as eight smaller 'Blister' hangars which could each accommodate a pair of Spitfires. These all made maintenance more comfortable for the fitters, though most of the aircraft were kept on the dispersal pads which were built around the edge of the perimeter track.

Summerfeld tracking, a metal mesh that was used in place of concrete for rapid construction, was used to create extra taxiways which would allow landing aircraft to quickly get off the runways and so increase the capacity of the airfield.

On March 1st 1942, RAF Boulmer was officially opened, by which time the staffing for the two airfields was nearly 1600 people. Boulmer would take on the role of advance training, with the pilots moving there part way through the course.

By now, training was in full swing with men regularly passing out as courses were completed, and new ones arriving. Flying time varied depending upon the weather, but on average, each pupil had about 20 hours a month in the air, predominately in Spitfires. In the early years, they would be flying the Spitfire Mk. I. Later, mark II and V aircraft would be allocated to training units, the regular upgrading of the front line aircraft ensuring a steady supply of older versions.

In all, there were 36 courses held in Northumberland, so 57 OTU must have trained over 1,000 Spitfire pilots during its time here. The last course, number 76, was suspended in May 1945 when the war in Europe ended, with its pupils being posted elsewhere.

On average a course would last about 12 weeks, though it would be up to four weeks before a pilot would take off in a Spitfire. There was a lot of ground instruction to get through, which included:

- Knowledge of Spitfires
- Handling the radio
- Cockpit drill and emergency procedures
- Oxygen system on Spitfires
- Readiness to fly Spitfires

There was a decompression chamber at Eshott where the new pilots could learn about the effects of low oxygen on the brain. Half of the group in the chamber would have oxygen masks and the others not. The ones with oxygen were able to observe the effects of high altitude flying without oxygen, as their comrades progressively showed the effects of oxygen starvation - over-confidence, giggling and an inability to carry out the simplest of tasks. It was a potent lesson.

Once the necessary tests had been passed, the new trainee would do a few hours in the two seat Miles Master with an Instructor. The Master was an advanced trainer, which bridged the gap between the Harvard and the Spitfire. Only when the Instructor was happy would they progress on to the single seat Spitfire. There were no two seat Spitfires during WW2 so it must have been a daunting experience to make a first flight in such a powerful machine with its specialised taxiing and landing technique.

It is worthwhile looking at the report of a typical course on its completion, taken from the Operations Record Book for March 1944. This gives a sense of what the training covered.

No. 58 Course passed out today. The course commenced [January 1944] with 43 pupils. 36 pupils passed out, the 7 wastage being disposed as follows:

1 Awaiting transfer

5 to No. 59 Course

1 Posted to 288 Squadron

Standard of flying: The standard of flying of No. 58 course was "Good Average"; 4 passed out "Above Average" and 13 "Good Average". The accident rate was poor - 7 avoidable and 1 unavoidable. One pilot was sent to ACRS and a French sergeant pilot was sent to the Free French Camp, Camberley for disciplinary purposes; the reason for this action being, in the first case, due to a careless landing, and in the second, for landing on the wrong runway and then taxiing against the traffic and colliding with another aircraft.

Night flying - "Average"; 2 accidents - the first a heavy landing causing a burst tyre, aircraft swing and the undercarriage collapsed; the second was a landing without wheels.

Average flying time for pupils were; Spitfire 54 hours Day, 4 hours Night. Master 2.45 hours Day, Nil Night.

Exercises: Formation carried out by this Course was 21.00 hours. General standard "Good Average". Aerobatics and general handling of aircraft - "Good Average".

Low Flying and Navigation: At least two low level 200 mile cross counties were undertaken by the pupils with an Instructor following in another Spitfire. The weather was rather better for this Course than the previous one. The Dominie was used for low level navigation by the Navigation Officer; and one high level cross country, 3000 feet, was done by each pupil.

Gunnery Training: Air to Air was "Average"; the percentage of hits being 1.0% machine guns and 1.0% cannons. Air to Ground was "Above Average" - 10.7%. Total number of bombs dropped - 15 per pupil; average error - 27 feet.

Bomber affiliation was only carried out once. 8 aircraft only being used.

Co-operation is not good, and no matter how hard we try with the Bomber Squadron, it just does not work out properly; and with 44 pupils and only three weeks, we cannot afford to keep the aircraft grounded waiting for the Halifaxes.

Interceptions: Nil

Standard of Ground Training: Attendance at lectures was 100%. Average hours Link and Hunt Trainer - 8.45 hours. All pupils did the Decompression Test with no trouble.

Discipline on the ground was "Average". Dinghy drill was carried out at least three times. The pupils visited Kenton Operations and Northsteads GCI; also Merchant Navy for a launching at Newcastle and the Air Sea Rescue at Blyth.

Owing to better weather, we were able to get the Course away before the correct date, and unfortunately, the Escape exercise was overlooked.

The skies around the two airfields would have been busy. Generally, between them, the two bases would achieve between 2,000 and 3,000 Spitfire flying hours every month. This would mean about ten Spitfires in the air each and every hour when flying was taking place. In addition, RAF Acklington was also very close by. It is unsurprising, therefore, that there were a number of accidents, including mid-air collisions, which often resulted in fatalities. Indeed, in the 2½ years that 57 OTU operated in Northumberland, there were 33 pupil pilots killed, an average of about one each month.

All accidents were thoroughly investigated but more often than not the cause was identified as pilot error which is perhaps inevitable considering that the trainees were flying machines more powerful than they would have experienced before. The following are just a selection of the fatal accidents that occurred:

27th February 1943; two pilots collided in mid-air while carrying out formation flying practice. A flight of four Spitfires were adjusting from line abreast to line astern. Number 2 slowed down too quickly and number 3 had to pass beneath to try to avoid a collision. Sadly, number 2 clipped it as it passed below, cutting off the rear section. Both aircraft crashed.

11th October 1943; a Spitfire crashed after carrying out 'dog fighting' practice. It is thought that the pilot may have blacked out due to severity of the manoeuvres.

12th April 1944; a Spitfire, piloted by a 19 year old Norwegian, while returning from a training mission, collided head on with an USAAF P47D Thunderbolt which was based at RAF Milfield, north of Wooler. The USAAF aircraft had been carrying out simulated attacks on a convoy on the Great North Road near Felton.

In all three cases, all the pilots involved were killed. Many of the pilots who died were buried at the cemetery at Chevington, alongside some of the Luftwaffe pilots who were shot down over Northumberland.

As well as fatalities, there were many other accidents. They were classified as 'avoidable' or 'unavoidable' as in the end of course report above. Unavoidables tended to be mechanical problems such as engine failure. Avoidables covered a much wider range, such as trying to take off with the propeller being set in coarse pitch, or a heavy landing. The attrition rate for aircraft at OTUs was very high.

In January 1944 RAF Milfield ceased OTU activities and as a result more training was thrown onto 57 OTU. By this time the airfield was mainly operating with Mk. Vb and Vc Spitfires.

RAF Eshott was shutdown on 15th May 1945, just a week after the end of the war in Europe. Course No. 75 passed out on that day, and No. 76 was suspended with the trainees being dispersed to other OTUs. Boulmer closed at the same time. The Spitfires were sent to Maintenance Units from where most were scrapped.

Appendix 5: **Exploring Wartime Remains**

Maps

An essential tool in exploring the military remains is an Ordnance Survey map, the most useful ones being the 1:50,000 Landranger series, and the more detailed 1:25,000 Explorer series.

Within this book, the locations of remains are described using Ordnance Survey map references. The map will also show you how you might reach the location, using tracks and footpaths for example. The maps themselves include instructions in how to read a map reference.

A 'four-figure' map reference, such as AB 12 34, will define a 1km x 1km square, which is useful for a large site such as an airfield. Smaller sites need more accuracy; a 'six-figure' reference, AB 123 456, is accurate to 100m x 100m. An eight-figure reference is accurate to 10m x 10m, though such accuracy will require a suitable GPS device rather than pure map reading skill to fix the location on the ground.

Access

In England, we do not have an automatic right to access any piece of land. Public rights of way (which include public footpaths, bridleways etc.) are marked on OS maps. Permissive rights of way, where the landowner has allowed access, are also usually identified on maps. High ground can often have open access, though there are few wartime sites in these areas; the Ottercops Moss radar site is one notable exception. Coastal areas, such as beaches, are often open access

To avoid trespass and confrontation with landowners, it is therefore important to determine what the access restrictions might be before visiting any site and requesting permission from the landowner where this is necessary. Access is rarely declined when politely requested.

Safety

It is probably stating the obvious, but most of the military remains mentioned in this book have not been maintained for many decades and as such can be dangerous places. There can also be dangerous excavations, such as drains, hidden by the undergrowth or by standing water. Care must always be taken when exploring around any sites.

It is also important to respect the importance of all these historic sites and to avoid any damage. There have been instances, for example, of individuals breaking into locked or sealed buildings, causing untold destruction.

Bibliography

Defending Britain; Twentieth Century Military Structures in the Landscape;
Osbourne M, Tempus 2004

The Military Airfields of Britain; Northern England; Delve K, Crowood 2006

Airfields of North-East England in the Second World War; Chorlton M, Countryside Books 2005

Air Crash Northumberland; Gray R, Corbett J, Shipley J, Anderson N, Countryside Books 2008

Almost Forgotten; The Search for Aviation Accidents in Northumberland, Volume 1;
Davies C, Amberley 2012

Almost Forgotten; The Search for Aviation Accidents in Northumberland, Volume 2;
Davies C, Wanney Books 2016

Action Stations; 7, Military Airfields of Scotland, the North-East and Northern Ireland;
Smith D, PSL 1983

Defensive Northumberland; Alexander C, Amberley 2018

North Northumberland at War 1939 – 1945; Armstrong C, Pen and Sword 2017

Northumberland Aviation Diary; Aviation Incidents from 1790 – 1999; Walton D, Norav 1999

Churchill's Underground Army; A History of the Auxiliary Units in WW2;
Warwicker J, Front Line Books 2008

**The Last Ditch; The Secrets of the Nationwide British Resistance Organisation and the Nazi Plans
for the Occupation of Britain 1940 – 1944**;
Lampe D Cassell 1968

Fields of Deception; Britain's Bombing Decoys of the Second World War;
Dobinson C, Methuen 2000

Building Radar; Forging Britain's Early-Warning Chain, 1935 – 1945; Dobinson C, Methuen 2010

Craster, Northumberland; An Archaeological Investigation of a World War II Radar Complex;
Hunt A and Ainsworth S, English Heritage 2006 (available as an internet download)

Cold War; Building for Nuclear Confrontation 1946 – 1989; Cockcroft W and Thomas J, English
Heritage 2003

Northern Northumberland's Minor Railways; Volume 1; Jermy R, Oakwood Press 2010

**Most Secret; Uncovering the Story of Northumberland's Underground Resistance – the Auxiliary
Units of WW2**; Hall I, Wanney Books 2015

Zeppelins Over the North East; The Airship Raids of WW1 Between the Tweed and Tees;
Hall I. Wanney Books 2014

Spitfires Over Northumberland; A Wartime Story of Acklington, Eshott and Boulmer;
Hall I, Wanney Books 2018

The Archaeology Data Service website has detailed reports on wartime remains at Druridge
(Defence Area 60) **and Wooler** (defence Area 76). Both reports are available as downloads.

**Volume 20 of Northumberland County Council's Archaeology in Northumberland has detailed
articles on the Heiferlaw Zero Station and the Bamburgh ROC post.**